ANTIQUE
BASKETS and BASKETRY

FRANCES THOMPSON

Cover Design: Geri Wolfe
Interior Layout: Mary Jane Strouf
Photographs by the Author

Library of Congress Catalog
Card Number 84-052054

ISBN 0-87069-427-8

10 9 8 7 6 5 4 3 2 1

Published by

Wallace=Homestead
publishers of fine books

Wallace-Homestead Book Company
580 Waters Edge
Lombard, Illinois 60148

One of the *ABC PUBLISHING* abc Companies

To
Darlene Mullen

❖ Contents ❖

History
of Baskets

Basketry is as young as tomorrow and as old as the records of mankind. Still today children in some summer camps and Bible schools are taught the art of basketry—a continuation of a craft practiced by all peoples for all times. Adults are also offered courses in basketmaking at some colleges. This education has been developed because of the growing popularity of old handmade baskets. As the demand for old baskets has increased, their supply has dwindled and their prices risen. Therefore many users of baskets have felt the need to learn to make their own.

The art of basketry was practiced by the early Egyptians, as witnessed by examples found in old tombs. Ancient Romans took great pride in their basket work, and the Britons were noted as basketmakers par excellence.

Baskets were so plentiful and so necessary that they are mentioned numerous times in the Bible. Probably the two most familiar of these would be Moses floating down the Nile in a covered basket made of bulrushes, and using a basket to "take up the fragments" after the multitudes had been fed on the five loaves and two fishes.

Baskets are so universally accepted that songs have been written about them. Do you remember "A Tisket, a Tasket?" For many years baskets have been mentioned in children's books. One of the most famous of these books is about Little Red Riding Hood who carried a basket over her arm as she went through the woods to her grandmother's house.

Baskets are certainly not a new invention, nor can any one country be credited with their discovery. Even the most uncivilized people such as the aborigines of Tasmania know the art of basketry. It is a delightful hobby or craft that lets each maker, regardless of his environment, find some material, free for the taking, with which to make baskets of his or her own design.

At one time or another, nearly all materials like willow, reed, honeysuckle vine, long pine needles, yucca, cattails, or splints from the oak, ash, hickory, or black elm trees have been used. In different countries various materials were used—whatever was available and free. For instance, in North Africa esparto grass was used "for all manner of basketmaking." In China and Japan, bamboo was the favorite; in India it was khuskhus grass and in the interior of Alaska, roots of evergreens were used. In the remote islands of the Aleutian chain the women made long, weary trips to gather roots and grasses suitable for making baskets. While traveling they searched for materials that could be used to dye the roots and grasses.

Around the turn of the present century it was considered fashionable for housewives to develop some artistic skills, or learn a craft. There was little or no work for them outside the home so some painted china, others pictures, some did needlework, and many learned the old art of basketry.

Making baskets was so popular at that time it was taught locally in various classes, learned by mail-order lessons, and some colleges, usually for women, offered classes. It is known that basketry was taught at Montevallo, formerly a college for "young ladies," located in central Alabama as late as half a century ago. A seventy-five-year-old lady remembers taking the course that taught pine-needle basketry. This was probably the most popular type of basketry because materials were plentiful in the area, and the work was different from the regular splint-and-cane basketry being done.

Some ladies engaged in basketmaking at that time could afford to purchase materials. Rather than gather willow branches or honeysuckle vines, they preferred to buy materials like cane and rattan, a kind of palm grown in the forests of India, and raffia from Madagascar. The latter two were imported into this country to support a growing business. On the farms and where money continued to be scarce, baskets were usually made of reed, vines, or splints.

The first Americans to master the art of basketry were of course the Indians. They not only used the well-known willow, reeds, pine needles, and vines, but also spruce roots, cedar bark, yucca, and Indian hemp. Today the latter materials would be of little use without the skilled hands of the Indian women.

The Indians and primitive men of all races waged wars and hunted while the women became the inventors, the mothers, the nurses, and the homemakers. It was the women who had to devise methods to furnish their family's needs—shelter, clothing, mats, and baskets. They mastered the intricacies of weaving so well that no modern craftsman with his machines has been able to add anything new.

Basketry was one of the most expressive of the Indian handicrafts. Into a basket a woman could weave the history, tradition, and folklore of her people. That is one of the reasons old Indian baskets are so sought after. They are of interest to the historian as well as to the collector. Much study and research is involved before the average collector can determine whether the design that looks like a flash of lightning means a mountain stream or an incoming tide. Small stars within a circle usually represent the constellation Corona. A spider web design could be a prayer for rain. Rattlesnake markings could also be a prayer, in this case, asking for protection for the weaver and her family from the deadly rattlesnake. The design could have been used for the same purpose by all the tribes, as the eastern Indians in the mountains were as wary of the timber rattler as the desert Indians were of the diamond-back.

The material and construction might be the same, but basketry items made by the various Indian peoples differed in both form and design. Often workmanship varied greatly. Some baskets were closely woven and others were coarse and poorly done. Then, as now, some people were more skilled in one area of the crafts than in another. At one time the Navajos were noted for their fine silversmiths and blanket weavers, and the Apaches for their fine basketry. Of course, the Paiutes, Navajos, and Pima, along with the Apaches, were known as good coil basketmakers.

One method of making coiled baskets required fine, ropelike withes of yucca wrapped with flat strips of the same plant. Starting at the bottom, the worker coiled the rope-shaped fibers around and around, attaching them by a method of weaving. This process continued until the basket had reached the desired dimensions. Baskets made this way were strong and compact. They were attractive when dyed in various colors. A similar process was used later to make baskets of rye or pine needles.

For the early Romans and Egyptians, as well as the American Indians and pioneers, basketry furnished innumerable essential articles for both home and field. We tend to think of basketry as the art of making an article to be used as a carrier or for storage. That was not always the case. Basketry is known to have been used to construct weirs, cradles, screens, canoes, novelties, helmets, and shields, as well as ceremonial articles, cooking vessels, and water jugs. Wicker furniture and accessories are simply a variation of basketry.

This shallow, round basket or tray was made from the leaves of the yucca plant. It was plaited or woven in a simple crosswise manner, then the rim wrapped with the leaves.

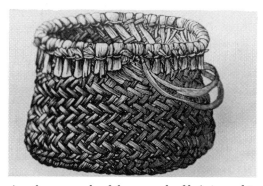

Another example of the yucca leaf being used to make a peach basket. This one dates back to before 1875.

Early baskets were used for such mundane chores as carrying corn, melons, and fruit from the fields. The Indians used the smaller baskets for storing shelled corn, beans, and the herbs and plants they used for medicine or dyes. Acorns, another staple food among some tribes, were not only gathered in baskets, but they were also cooked in baskets.

Acorns are very bitter unless they are boiled. The women gathered the acorns, brought them home, and cooked them by adding hot stones to the water in a water-tight basket. The water was kept boiling by the addition of more hot stones. After boiling, when the bitterness was gone, the acorns could be dried and pounded into meal.

At least one researcher felt that pottery may have been discovered through the cooking-basket method. Her theory was that a hungry husband arrived home and demanded dinner. His harassed wife, trying to hurry the cooking process, coated her cooking basket with clay so she could place it directly over the fire. When the meal was over she could have discovered that not only did she still have her cooking basket, but an earthenware pot as well. The theory may be all wrong, but it does have possibilities.

Two unusual basket-type articles were devised to aid in the nut and acorn harvest. These will probably be difficult to find today, but are well worth the search. One is a spoon-shaped woven scoop used to gather nuts under the piñon trees in the Rocky Mountains. Being not only skilled artisans, but also responsible for the family food supply, the women designed and made a scoop that fitted their needs. With the long handle they could run the scoop along the ground. Then by shaking it, the dirt would fall through the coarse, sievelike bottom, leaving the nuts.

Since every Indian woman was her own miller, she had to devise ways to save all the precious meal. To achieve this goal she wove a bottomless, bowl-shaped basket, which she placed on her favorite rock—one worn and hollowed from much grinding. Then into the basket she poured the grain, acorns, or nuts. With a stone pestle inserted through the basket, she ground the contents very fine without the wind blowing any of it away. These pieces are also extremely scarce today.

It has been said that necessity is the mother of invention and chances are, it was never more true than in those early days. Without buckets or pails as we know them, it was necessary for the Indians who lived

Two sides of a basket made in the Great Smoky Mountains are shown. Since both the mountaineers and the Cherokees used the same methods, the basket could easily have been made by either.

in the desert areas of the Southwest to invent some type of container to carry water and to hold it once they were home. So they made a waterproof jug in basketry. Usually globular-shaped with small necks, they were closely woven, then coated with a resin or gum.

Like the later pottery water jugs, these basket jugs had small horsehair ears or loops attached to the sides so strings or ropes could be passed through, allowing the jug to be carried on the head or over the shoulders. Larger water jugs could be tied together and placed over the back of a horse if the water had to be carried for a long distance.

Some researchers credit the very early, woven water jugs to the Apaches, as they were one of the most skilled in the art of basketry. Before the turn of the century, excellent examples of old baskets could be found in any village, but it was thought the finer examples in some villages could have arrived through the medium of barter. The Paiutes were another tribe well-known for their waterproof jugs made of willow and coated with gum from the piñon tree. The Paiutes traded their jugs to the Navajos for their famous woven blankets. It is thought the Havasupais designed the first stand-up water jugs or baskets. These jugs were woven with a tapered point that could be stuck in the ground, thus preventing the jug from overturning and spilling the water.

The eastern Cherokees didn't have the water problems encountered by the people in the arid areas of the Southwest, but they did make waterproof baskets. These were double woven of rivercane, then coated with beeswax.

Although the Cherokees could and did use other materials in their basketmaking, their favorites were rivercane, white oak, and willow. Even today they will not use metal in their baskets. Freeswinging handles are carved entirely from wood and lids are installed on a dowel-type hinge.

Apparently all Indians made some type of flat or saucer-shaped bowl in basketry for use in storing meal and fine grain. Another similar, larger basket was used for winnowing grain or seeds. This task was accomplished by placing a small amount of grain in the basket, and with a skillful motion throwing it into the wind, then catching the grain as it fell. This process was continued until the chaff was separated from the grain.

Baskets were an absolute necessity in the early Indian homes. They were not only used to carry water, harvest and cook food, winnow and grind grain, nuts, and acorns, but they were also heaped with gifts to appease the wrath of an angry god. They were used by gamblers to toss the dice. At wedding feasts and ceremonial dances they were a must. When a member of the family died, baskets of food were placed on the grave so the deceased could eat until he reached another world.

Each person used whatever materials were available to him or her. For instance, yucca was readily available to the Zuni and Hopi so they used it to construct some of their most interesting baskets. As willow usually grew near their source of water, and sooner or later everyone had to go there, the use of willow was universal. The Menomini made strips or splints from the plentiful black elm of Wisconsin for their baskets. Limbs three to four inches in diameter were hammered with a wooden mallet until the individual layers of the branch were detached from the layer immediately beneath it. The layers were cut into narrow strips with a crude native knife, and rolled into coils until needed.

The Pilgrims who landed in America were well-versed in the art of basketry. Through an exchange of ideas with the Indians, both the Pilgrims and the Indians came up with some good ideas and fine examples of basketry. In fact a report shows that in 1675 one man listed among his choice possessions a "Wikker Flasket," which was later identified as a woven hamper. The early settlers also used basketry to make traps at the pond outlets to catch fish, and containers for sowing seeds.

In those days the quality of the household and the ability of the housewife was judged, to a certain extent, by the number of

Hopi basketmaker at work (from old illustration).

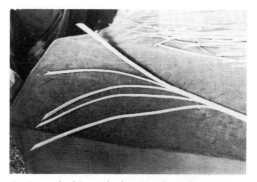

A piece of white oak showing how the splints are first cut with a knife, then peeled off.

Oak splints are being woven into a basket. A skilled basketmaker can prepare enough material for one basket in a day, although work continued until there was usually enough for a dozen or more baskets. Approximately one day is required to make a simple basket of average size.

featherbeds in the home. Then the beds were judged by the kind of feathers they contained, with goose down rating tops. Next in order came feathers from the hen, turkey, owl, and hawk. The goose's feathers could be plucked two to three times a year if the housewife could endure the loud squawking and painful pecking. Naturally it became essential to devise ways and means of getting the feathers or down with as little trouble as possible. Some held the goose's head and neck under the picker's arm, others pulled a long woolen stocking over its head. The more ingenious women made woven baskets that fit perfectly over the goose's head and neck. The goose might continue to squawk, but it couldn't peck, and was in no danger of smothering. A basket was also made to hold the feathers so they could air dry.

Most of these old examples would be difficult if not impossible to find now. But many lovely baskets from around the turn of the present century are available with probably the so-called gizzard-shaped or buttocks baskets the most popular in the East, and the Indian baskets the most sought after in the West. All types of old splint, willow, and reed baskets, made either by the white man or by the Indian, are now standard stock in many antique shops, shows, and malls. And for those not too concerned with age, but who collect baskets for beauty and excellent workmanship, there is a bonanza today in the Indian arts and crafts mutuals and trading posts as well as the arts and crafts shows being held all around the country during the spring, summer, and fall.

Basketry is as important to the Indians today as it was a century ago, but for a different reason. Then baskets were made for personal use or for barter. Today they are made for the express purpose of selling to help supplement incomes. As one Cherokee basketmaker explained it, "I have always made and sold baskets. I needed the money to raise my children. Fifteen or twenty years ago I was lucky to get prices like $.50 to $1.50 for my baskets. Now I am getting from $40 to $300 a basket depending on size and workmanship. It is a pleasure to make baskets now when people appreciate them."

And it is not only the Indians who are supplementing their incomes with basketry. Many students and teachers from basketry classes around the country along with others who still remember learning basketmaking from their parents have joined in the explosive revival of basketry. They all exhibit and sell their wares at the area arts and crafts shows. They, too, are pleased when their work is praised or purchased. Prices on these baskets run from around $10 for small, sometimes poorly made examples, to as much as $300 for excellent pieces.

With the ever-increasing interest in baskets, chances are that prices will go even higher in the future. There are few bargains in basketry today, but there are some excellent examples of the craft available.

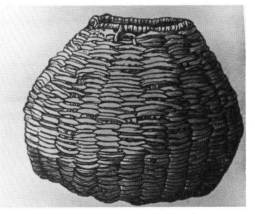

Coarse willow basket attributed to the Zuni.

Well-designed and skillfully woven baskets similar to this one held the finest ground meals and flour.

Coiled or wrapped-type basket made of grapevines.

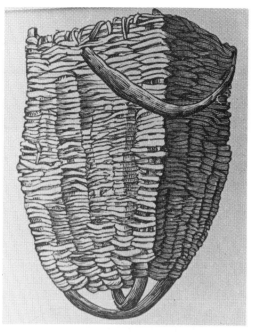

Around 1880 baskets like this carried fruits, mostly peaches, from the fields.

Birch bark basket thought to have been used for berry picking. Fabric handle on side.

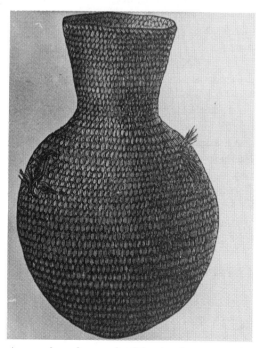

A vase-shaped example of the closely woven water jug or basket.

An older (circa 1870), finer quality, woven water jug.

New rivercane baskets made by the Cherokees with the same methods, materials, and dyes as their ancestors used for hundreds of years. The baskets are hanging on a piece of uncut rivercane.

A cornmeal basket or tray from the Wolpi village was made of willow colored with vegetable dyes.

Tall handle allowed a berry picker to drop berries in this splint basket without difficulty.

Early Cherokee basket and the old flint knife used to cut the splints.

Willow meal basket dyed with vegetable dyes.

Cherokee-made fish basket.

Both mountaineers and Cherokees made this type covered basket using white oak splints.

Late coiled piece made of leaves.

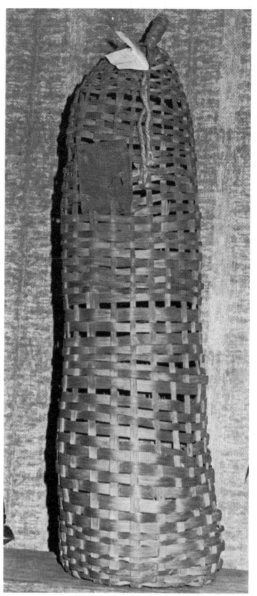

Later fish basket thought to have been made by white man.

Made of roots, probably spruce.

White oak splint basket made by Cherokees for storing vegetables and grain.

Rivercane basket with wrapped handle. The Choctaws made some baskets of this type.

This loosely woven tray was used by the Cherokees to sift ground corn, removing the husks from the meal.

Poorly made vine basket, probably similar to the early "Wikker Flasket."

Basket made of black elm.

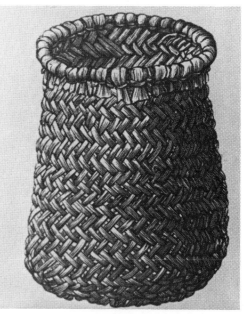

Peach basket made of yucca leaves, circa 1875.

Shaped like a bowl, nevertheless it was called a basket by the Indians who made it to hold finely ground meal and other things.

Late coiled basket made of leaves.

Basket that had been left in an attic for fifty years.

Rye basket.

Large handmade willow basket.

Same basket as it looked one year later after it was allowed to "age" by hanging outside.

Basket was used for sewing basket.

Woven splint doll sofa.

Solid birch-bark basket, apple basket, and coiled vine basket.

Bottom of basket.

Splint basket with walnut-dyed design.

Display of baskets on shelves.

Baskets displayed on old towel rack.

Artificial flowers in old basket.

Open sewing basket.

Picnic basket with plates, cups, flatware, place mats, and napkins.

Dried and artificial flowers in old basket.

Basket of hand towels for bathroom.

Grouping of baskets.

Baskets grouped on table.

Potted pocketbook plant in old basket.

Potted shamrock plant in hanging basket.

Basket filled with wooden cooking tools and quilted pot holders.

Rivercane basket full of peaches.

Decorated Christmas balls in basket.

Eggs and berries in basket.

Blue and white Christmas balls in old basket.

Christmas greenery and candy canes in new handmade basket.

24

❖ 2 ❖

Basket Materials

A list of the materials used in basketry over the years would read like the who's who of field and forest. Man's ingenuity is such that he has devised ways to use whatever is available in whatever way is needed. He is a survivor and his use of available materials to fit whatever job is at hand is about all the proof needed to make the point.

Generally he uses whatever is most plentiful and easiest to obtain in his own area. For instance, bamboo, which reaches heights of fifty to eighty feet and a diameter of ten feet, was used in the majority of baskets made in the Orient. Willow was the favorite in France and England. In New Zealand flax was more popular. In South America, Africa, and the East Indies palm leaves were used extensively. If any one material was more universally used in early America it was willow, with splints from various trees running a close second. In later years it seems the process was reversed with splints becoming more popular.

Baskets can be made of practically any material, and as proof of that a 90-year-old basketmaker made this one using metal bottle caps and burrs from a sweet gum tree.

Then she made this one by gluing seeds over a base and adding a border and handle of burrs from the sweet gum tree.

It was possible to gather a variety of the basket materials without harming the plant life in any way. In many cases the removal of old vines and roots helped the tree or vine by allowing space for new growth. However, if tree limbs were cut it was a different matter.

In the East it was the custom to "chip" the tree to check the desirability for basket-making materials. If the chips from the oak would break rather easily, and the grain was such that it would split nicely when cut with a knife, it was considered ideal for basketmaking. The disadvantage was that when the trees were chipped and found unsatisfactory, they were left to die from the chipping.

Much care was taken in gathering materials to make baskets of excellent quality. The gathering of the right type of materials and their preparation were almost as important as the quality of work-manship. The Cherokees still stress that wild honeysuckle vines should be gathered each fall, and then only that year's growth should be taken. This young growth is small and free of sprouts or branches, at least the ones that will leave a permanent mark on the vine after it is prepared. When the vines are allowed to grow for two years or more, the removal of the sprouts or branches leaves knots along the vines that detract from the smoothness of the basket. One old-time basketmaker emphasized that one sure way to identify buckbush baskets from middle and western Tennes-see was to look for excessive amounts of knots on the vines. Apparently, basket-makers in those areas gathered the older vines.

Buckbush, also known as coralberry, coral bush, and Indian currant, is a small bush that grows over much of the Eastern and Southern parts of the United States. Once the scraggly vines are soaked and peeled, the material resembles honey-suckle vine. It is difficult for the average person to see the difference. In fact, most of the old vine baskets are so similiar it takes a person experienced in vine culture to distinguish which vines were used, especially when they have been made up into baskets for many years. And it was not unusual for the maker to use two or more different kinds of vines in one basket. The vines might be similar with a different type adding a decorative touch. Perhaps that is the charm of basketry—every maker used whatever was at hand to create an entirely different basket each time.

Unless you decide to become a connois-seur of old basket materials, several sim-ple categories such as roots, vines, bark, splints, grasses, pine needles, and leaves will suffice.

There may be others in the root category, but the most commonly used were the roots of the alder, bracken, elm, cedar, red fir, hemlock, rush, black locust, mulberry, yucca, willow, and sassafras. Also, the black, white, and red spruces, digger, sugar, Georgia, and yellow pines were popular choices.

Using two separate parts of the plant or tree was not unusual. In the case of some pines both the roots and needles were used. The willow was another example, with both the roots and branches being used. The mulberry was very versatile as basketmak-ers soon found. They could use the twigs, roots, or bark to make baskets, but not a combination.

In some areas of the South, baskets made of vines are more treasured, probably because they are not as plentiful as others. Since most vines with runners were accept-able, old basketmakers gathered ivy, cross-vine, clematis, smilax, and wisteria as well as honeysuckle and grapevine. In areas where grapevines grew wild, basketmakers had only to trek through the forest to obtain enough basketmaking material to last all winter.

Basketmakers in each section of the country soon found available trees whose bark was easily adaptable to basketry. Some were only useful as spokes, others made excellent weavers, but in most cases one type bark could be cut coarse for spokes while the finer-cut pieces were used for weaving. Again, some varieties may have been missed, but it is known that the following were used: basswood, birch, cedar, (both red and white), hazel or hazelnut (a very popular material), yew, redbud, sassafras, Indian hemp (also called dogbane in some areas), white pine, Oregon maple, black walnut, vine maple, and mulberry.

Judging by the number of old baskets that have survived, it would appear that splint baskets made from trees like elm, hickory, ash, maple (red, white, or swamp), and white oak were the most popular. In researching we found the term "white oak" overworked. It is not likely that every splint basket from Ohio to the Gulf of Mexico was made of one specific type of oak. The term did seem to be used more frequently in Tennessee, Kentucky, and North Carolina. However, it is doubtful that most people could distinguish between the various oak trees after the splints had been cut and aged for years.

In an effort to further verify this trend, we checked an old botany book and found there are twenty-two different types of oak trees growing in the United States. Is it possible any one person would be able to distinguish the difference between old splints cut from a live oak, willow oak, upland willow oak, laurel oak, swamp laurel oak, water oak, barren oak, iron oak, downy black oak, scrub barren oak, bear oak, red oak, pine oak, Spanish oak, black oak, yellow bark oak, scarlet oak, white oak, swamp chestnut oak, red chestnut oak, chestnut oak, and just plain old swamp white oak?

The scarcity of old baskets created by their rising popularity has seen the introduction of "aged" baskets on the market. This in turn has caused some controversy over the "color" old baskets should have. Some argue they should be a dark grayish brown color while others think they should be a golden brown. Both are right as baskets age different shades in different parts of the country. It is believed that the climate has much to do with it.

Splint basket influenced by New England and maybe Shaker styles.

Of course the type of tree from which the splint was cut probably has lots of bearing on color, but it is almost certain that climate has more impact. For instance, baskets from the hot, humid Southern part of the country will have aged to a sort of golden brown in about the same time required for them to have turned a grayish brown in the damp, cooler sections of the country.

Or if the baskets are kept in the dark they won't age at all. A few years ago a basket was found in the attic of a southern Alabama home. It was exactly the color it had been when first made. The elderly owner remembered a family member making the basket about fifty years before. Buried beneath clothing, carpets, and other items stored in the attic, it is doubtful light had touched the basket since it was stored away shortly after being made.

Testing has been done in both the hot, humid areas as well as the cool, damp areas, using new splint baskets made as nearly as possible from the same materials. They were put outside and left for nearly a year. By that time the ones in the hot, humid areas had turned a golden brown while those in the cooler, damp climate had turned a dark grayish brown— about the same colors as the old baskets from each area.

One person offered the opinion that even with fast aging, it was easy for her to determine which baskets were old and which were new simply by looking for the loose hairlike strings that are part of the splints. This is not necessarily true because many of the makers of new baskets know the tricks of the trade used by the older basketmakers, such as holding the newly made basket over a lighted candle to burn off the hairlike strings.

The opinion that older baskets were better made than the new ones also has flaws. There have been skilled and unskilled workers since time immemorial. A century ago skilled crafts men and women took time to prepare the splints and then wove baskets of excellent quality, while others "split 'em and put 'em together." The same applies to today's makers.

Some of today's basketmakers are equally as skilled as those of a century ago, and probably work at their trade harder because they know that if the basket is of excellent quality, it will sell for big bucks. This is incentive enough. In the old days a basket was going to be used for everyday chores around the house or farm, and the maker got only satisfaction from the use of his basket. If it was to be sold, he might have ended up taking a dozen eggs or a chicken for his work. So he really wasn't into perfection that much.

Chances are, some of the same aging methods that were being used a decade ago are being used on baskets of poor quality today. When interest in old baskets began to soar and prices skyrocketed, there weren't enough of the old ones to go around. So a few devious methods were used to age new ones. The baskets might be soaked in very thin, light wood stain, or maybe boiled in a solution of tea or coffee. Some baskets were seen that appeared to have been lightly sprayed with a greenish gray paint resembling army khaki more than the patina of old baskets. During the past few years collectors have become more interested in other types of baskets, probably because of the prices of some of the old ones.

There are also those who argue that only new baskets will have nails in the handles and possibly in the rim. Again, this is not necessarily true as some of the old ones also had nails. It all depended on the area or the skills or the whims of the basketmaker.

Another factor that could greatly influence the color of a naturally aged basket is the material used. For example, it could have been made from the heart of the oak tree, which is somewhat darker than the outside or wood that is nearest the bark. Old-timers say baskets made of the heart of the oak are almost as dark when new as if the splints had been dyed with sumac. Since our ancestors were definitely not a wasteful people, they surely used the heart of the oak as well as the outside, which means there are plenty of those baskets out there. Some of the makers might have preferred using the darker woods to dyeing the splints. This would certainly explain why some baskets are darker than others.

The old baskets will always hold a soft spot in the basket collector's heart, but with so many fine quality new baskets coming on the market today, the majority will accept a few of the best mixed in with the old. Perhaps they think of them as the antiques of tomorrow. At least they know their history and have talked to their makers. The new ones are also excellent for study and comparison. When you consider today's prices on both, the new ones are a bargain.

Although the splint baskets seem to be very popular in most areas, baskets made of grasses and stems are also favored. Among the most valued of these in the East is the rivercane still used by both the Choctaw and Cherokee Indians; bulrushes, which have been used in basketry since the days of Moses; sedge grass, which is equally as useful in making baskets as in making dye for wool; beach grass, broomcorn, tule, wire grass, reed grass, bear grass, milkweed—both red and white—basket rush, Indian reed, rice grass, cattails, rabbit brush, sumac, maidenhair fern, and sage. Coconut palm leaves were also used.

Basket made of small twigs and branches after the style of the so-called Adirondack furniture.

New pine needle basket.

Old pine needle basket.

Basket made of assorted materials including grass.

Basket made of bamboo.

Basket made of palm leaves, late.

Buckbush basket made by unskilled basketmaker.

Basket made of vines woven over oak spokes.

Basket appears to have been made from wild honeysuckle vines.

Bottom of same basket showing workmanship.

Vine basket with damaged handle.

Rivercane basket.

Two sizes of the ever-popular, splint, gizzard-shaped or buttocks baskets.

The gizzard-shaped or buttocks baskets are among the most expensive in some areas, but damage like that around the rim will affect prices greatly. Only prime examples bring top dollar.

Basket made of hickory splints.

Fifty-year-old basket of grass and reed.

Basket made of an unknown type reed.

Excellent oak splint basket with decorative band just below the rim.

31

Basket of dyed ash.

Grapevine basket that has been painted.

Basket of fine reed.

Well-made utility basket of oak splints.

Worn handle shows this basket has been used.

Shopping basket made of ash splints and braided sweet grass.

Basket made of seeds and wire.

3

Dyes for Baskets

Even if dyes had been available, early American basketmakers probably would have hesitated to spend their limited "hard cash" on them. They could use vegetation from the fields and forests to make dyes at no cost. Actually, few mountain basketmakers used dyes in the early days. But as they began to have more spare time, they did begin using color.

In those times, as well as now, people wanted their possessions to be at least slightly different from those of their neighbors. No doubt this influenced them to use more colors in baskets. With rather drab log cabins, clothing, and surroundings, any addition of color was an improvement. Forget that the baskets would be used for chores around the house and farm, at least give them color. The bright colors in the baskets probably brightened their days and made the work go faster.

The Indians had used colors in their baskets for years, but it was not until the turn of this century that the average basketmaker began to use colors extensively.

When basketmaking experienced its revival around the turn of the present century, the ladies living in towns and cities began looking for hobbies—something to do during the long afternoons other than visiting. Along with other arts and crafts, these ladies began making baskets—all kinds of baskets. They could learn from books of instructions and classes held in the larger cities. "Store boughten" dyes probably colored their baskets because they didn't know how to make vegetable dyes. But the ladies in the rural areas continued to gather the vegetable-dye materials.

Those same vegetables for dyes are as readily available today as they were a century ago—provided you know where and for what to look. Although the average collector will never make a basket, learning about the dyes and how they were prepared yields a greater appreciation for the baskets in their own collections.

There is also the chance new dyes will be discovered by beginners in basketry, from plant materials easily found and used. Only recently, while experimenting, one basketmaker discovered that the pigment in purple iris will dye rattan almost as dark a shade as the blossom itself. The faded flower contains a purple liquid that can be rubbed on the rattan. The result is a beautiful purple color as long-lasting as that from any other dye.

In some basketry classes today commercial dyes designed for fabric are being used. Most of the baskets seen lately are in pastel colors that are completely out of character with old splint baskets. The baskets are being made of prepared reeds and splints, which limits basketmaking to the simple job of weaving. It is unknown whether the pastel colors will last with time and light. But it is suspected they will fade into oblivion when the baskets age to darker colors.

Originally purple dyes were obtained from logwood chips that had to be boiled to extract the color. Logwood is a tropical tree grown primarily in Central America.

Before any materials could be dyed satisfactorily, they had to be fixed overnight in a solution of three ounces of alum dissolved in one quart of water. The materials, splints, rivercane, vines, or others were then soaked for several hours in the logwood solution. A bluish purple, rather than a deep purple, was obtained by adding ammonia and baking soda to the solution.

Black dye was also made from logwood chips, but walnut bark, when available, was preferred by basketmakers because it was easier to use. Walnut could be used alone, but the logwood had to be mixed in a solution of fifty parts logwood to ten parts fustic, a tropical American tree of the mulberry family.

Logwood chips were invaluable in making several colors. All that was necessary was a change in the preparation. A yellowish brown could be obtained by boiling the logwood chips for fifteen minutes. The basket materials were then soaked in this solution for a short time, while watching constantly. When the desired shade was reached, they were removed immediately. This was one of the few dyes that didn't require an alum and fixing bath first.

A bright yellow dye could be made from the fustic, the same material used with logwood to make black dye. Used alone, the fustic chips were soaked overnight in enough water to cover them. The next day the container, complete with chips and water, was boiled for fifteen to twenty minutes. Longer boiling would turn it into a dark olive-green shade. A slightly different process was used with this solution. The material that had been fixed was dipped in and out of the solution until the desired shade was reached. A few dips would result in light yellow, more dippings a medium yellow, and long sessions in the dye pot would result in a golden or dark yellow.

Now the Cherokees use a plant they call yellow root to dye white oak splints for basketmaking. As far as is known, yellow root wasn't used by the old basketmakers, but it is possible they used sumac and sedge to create a yellow dye.

The ingredients used by the old-timers to make red dye might be a bit difficult to obtain now as they used cochineal (a dye made from the bodies of insects). Before using that dye the material was fixed in a solution of six parts stannous chloride crystals to four parts cream of tartar. They then were dipped into the dye made by boil-

Some of the roots and barks used by early settlers and Indians to dye baskets. Small plant on left is yellow root; only the root is necessary to make the dye. Next is bloodroots or pacoon roots used to make an orangy color. Bark on left is butternut, used to make a light brown. The other is walnut bark, used to make both black and brown.

ing and straining the cochineal. Today the Cherokees say they use little red dye on their baskets; but when they do, a commercial dye is used, their only concession to modernization in basketry.

In most areas, native dyes are still used on native materials. In the Great Smoky Mountain area the Cherokees continue to search for the roots and barks gathered by their ancestors. For black dye they use walnut bark (weaker solutions will also produce brown), yellow is obtained from yellow root, and butternut will produce a soft brown. A reddish purple is obtained from pokeberry juice, and to get an orangy color they use bloodroot, often called pacoon by the natives.

For those who preferred a natural or slightly colored finish on baskets, several solutions worked well. One was a polish made by simply mixing two parts turpentine to one part varnish.

To make the basket materials slightly darker than their natural color, they could be rubbed thoroughly with a mixture of three parts linseed oil and one part turpentine. A still darker color could be obtained by rubbing the materials with a mixture of four parts linseed oil, two parts turpentine, and one part cherry stain. To make the work easier, the materials were rubbed or treated with the dyes or polishes before weaving. The added advantage to this method was that the materials were thoroughly covered, giving a uniform appearance.

Several green finishes or polishes were used. To make a basic green finish, malachite green stain was added to a mixture of twelve parts turpentine and nine parts linseed oil. For a green polish, a few drops of malachite green were added to a mixture of two parts turpentine and one part varnish. The shade of green was varied by adding a little more or a little less color.

A color known as terra-cotta was made by adding a few drops of cherry stain to a mixture of twenty-one parts turpentine and five parts light oil finish. Since the light oil finish was a product of nearly a century ago, it is probably no longer available, but any good oil finish or polish would probably work as a substitute. Chances are, a different proportion of ingredients would have to be worked out to get the best results, and this would all depend upon the type of finish used. With some experience and luck a terra-cotta color similar to that used by the Western Indians could be made. That color combined with black was most effective on baskets.

Many of the baskets used in the illustrations in this chapter are new baskets, to show how bright the colors are originally. The colors will fade with age, but are vivid when new.

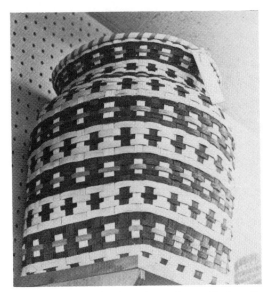

New oak-splint basket shows how effective the dyed designs can be.

Coiled basket dyed after the Indian style.

Old, dyed rivercane basket.

Different design and weave in old rivercane basket.

36

New honeysuckle basket dyed with walnut bark.

New spruce-root basket colored with vegetable dyes.

New double-woven rivercane basket dyed with vegetable dyes.

New oak-splint basket dyed with pokeberry juice and walnut bark.

Another Cherokee-made splint basket with a different design.

Two new Cherokee-made baskets show the range of styles.

New splint basket uses three colors, natural, butternut, and bloodroot.

4

Instructions for Making Baskets

With so many basketry classes being taught in junior colleges and basketmaking demonstrations at restorations around the country, many people at least know the fundamentals of basketmaking. But in an effort to increase the appreciation for older baskets, it seems necessary to show how it was done a century or so ago. The basics were the same as now, but the makers usually gathered their materials from the woods and the fields and worked long hours getting them ready for weaving or coiling.

Around the turn of the century when basketry along with several other arts and crafts was experiencing an explosive revival, several books were published with instructions for making all types of baskets and basketry items. The books, geared more to the city folk who were getting interested in basketry, listed the necessary materials and suggested they could be bought at the local basket factory. This indicated factories produced machine-made baskets in most key areas.

More than likely the rural folk wouldn't have read the books, even if they had been gifts. They didn't need them. Basketry was considered a craft in most families, one with instructions passed from one generation to another at an early age. It was customary for children to be making baskets on their own by the time they were five or six years old, according to one old-time basketmaker. The children went to the woods and fields with their parents to gather materials, and were soon as adept at gathering the right materials as the parents.

According to most of the instruction books, rattan was the most commonly used material if supplies were bought rather than gathered. Rattan came in round or flat strips in various sizes numbered from one to fifteen. Numbers two, three, and four were recommended as the best sizes for smaller baskets, while five and six were ideal for scrap baskets or wastebaskets.

The further you delve into the instruction books, the more apparent it becomes that they were really intended for the city dwellers. Farmers were not about to spend good money on what they considered inferior basket materials when they could get the superior materials free.

The principles of basketry are the same regardless of the materials used. At least one textbook has been found on basketry, but it is suspected it was used in city schools, not rural schools. Children who attended rural schools in those days were lucky if they could attend school as much as three or maybe four months out of the year. Their parents would never have permitted them to study a subject as commonplace as basketry in school. Why should they, when the children probably knew more about baskets by the time they started to school than the writers of the books? Schooltime was for learning to read, write, and cypher.

Rural children as well as many in the city literally cut their teeth on basketry—the sides of a woven willow cradle.

Raffia, also spelled raphia in some of the old books, is another material that has long been used in basketry. It is the outer cuticle of a palm. The pale yellow or almost natural-colored material is soft and pliable, which makes it easy for beginners to handle. Raffia came in single strips and braided. Today it is being used exclusively to make pine needle baskets and probably other coiled types.

Flat and braided rush was also imported for those wishing to buy materials. It came in natural colors of dull green or soft wood-browns. All these materials could be colored with home dyes "to weave baskets in the Indian manner," according to the instructions. Braided rush was especially recommended for work, flower, and candy baskets. For the basketmakers who preferred to gather native materials, the leaves of the cattail were recommended as an excellent substitute for the imported rush.

Tools used in basketry have always been quite simple—a pair of strong scissors, a yardstick, and a pail of water. For pine needle baskets a few ordinary drinking straws are necessary so short lengths can be cut off as needed to hold the pine needles in place and keep the coils uniform. Native or prepared basket materials were necessary as was a large needle when making "sewed" or coiled baskets.

The instruction books divided baskets into two types—coiled or sewn and woven. They also suggested the coiled type was easier, therefore best, for the beginner. Raffia made a better filling or rope so beginners were urged to use it coiled in their first baskets. Since work on the coil could progress as the basket was being constructed, it was not necessary to complete the coil in the beginning. Starting about an inch from the end, the worker wrapped the tightly wound coil of raffia loosely with a strand of raffia thread that had been threaded into a large needle. When sufficient wrapping had been completed, the coil was "turned on itself," and the needle was put directly through the twisted coil and sewed securely. As the coil was wrapped around and around, it was sewn or wrapped every one-fourth inch with the stitches always pointing toward the center.

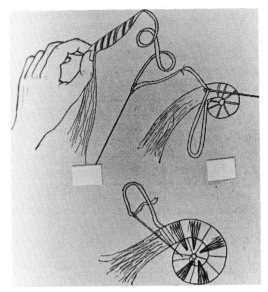

Illustration from 1904 book of basketry instructions, showing how the coils are wrapped and stitched.

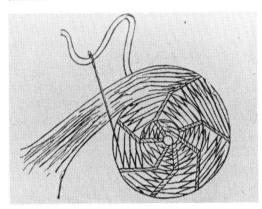

Close-up of coiled base.

The same principal was used to make pine needle baskets, but it has become more sophisticated in recent years. Actually there is less work preparing the pine needles than any other basket materials. The only thing necessary is to gather the dried long pine needles that may drop in your own yard, cut off the ends, and begin work. You can gather green needles, but they must dry in a dark, dry place for about six weeks. Otherwise they will shrink after the basket is made. The green needles have an entirely different color and are pretty when used alone or mixed with the older, dried, brown needles.

Pine needles are also used for decorative touches in the coiled baskets made by the Gullahs who live along the coast from Georgia through South Carolina. The basic material in the Gullah-made baskets is long grass that grows near the coast and along the edges of marshes in that area. It is often called "sea straw" by the people who make the baskets.

The worker fills a short portion of a drinking straw with pine needles or sea straw, depending on the size coil desired. He or she then starts coiling and sewing. Since the pine needles are different lengths they will be used up at intervals. This is good because as one length disappears, another is added. By adding at intervals, the basket is strengthened.

Naturally the strength of any basket depends on the quality of workmanship. For a stronger basket the coils should be wound tightly and the stitches placed closely.

After the worker has mastered the simple fundamentals of coiled basketry, variations are limitless. Many materials could be used, but the color and use (stitches) of the raffia could and did alter the appearance of the basket more than any other one factor. Indeed, many different stitches with assorted colors of raffia or thread will give baskets the appearance of having been made by Western Indians.

One ingenious soul of perhaps a century ago undoubtedly had problems getting her coiled basket started, that is, turning the coil on itself. She crocheted a small bottom using embroidery thread in a rainbow of colors. Modern pine needle basketmakers now often make lacy centers of raffia for trays if an especially decorative design is needed.

For woven baskets, the single weaving, over-and-under type, is the simplest form and the one most commonly used. Double weaving uses the same method except that two weavers or strips are used at once. This is an attractive weave when using contrasting colors. Triple weaving works the same way with three weavers or strips being

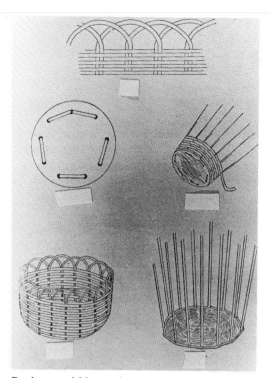

Baskets could be made using a wooden or woven base, but were usually finished like the top design.

placed behind three consecutive spokes and worked in succession.

Bottoms or bases for woven baskets could be made of stiff cardboard—although seldom used, thin basswood, plywood, or spokes. The last was most commonly used, but occasionally, baskets will be found with wooden bottoms. Using the wooden base created problems because holes for the spokes had to be drilled. This was somewhat difficult for the ladies. Once the spokes were securely in place weaving could begin. When the basket had reached the desired height, the spokes were fastened one over the other to form an attractive looped top. It was not necessary for all the wooden-based baskets to be round in shape, other shapes worked as well. The same applied to handles since some baskets were made with over-the-top handles and some were fastened on the sides. A number of basketry items didn't have handles at all.

In some areas, especially among the Shakers and the Nantucket lightship basketmakers, forms were used to shape the baskets. In many instances this method was employed because the baskets would serve as measures. So they had to be made accurately. This type was also easily stacked, one inside the other, when not in use.

During the revival period one of the most popular, and one of the most simple to make, of the fully woven baskets was the open work candy basket. The materials needed for this one were twenty-four pieces of No. 2 rattan, each cut to thirty inches long, and two No. 2 rattan weavers. The rattan was soaked until pliable, then the twenty-four pieces were separated into groups of six each. The first group was laid on the table in a vertical position. The second group was placed horizontally across the first at the exact center, the third group crossed the other two diagonally with its upper end to the right of the upper part of the vertical group. The next group was laid across the other, diagonally from the left to the upper part of the vertical group, and to the right of the lower part.

A weaver of No. 2 rattan was doubled around the upper end of the vertical group with its end toward the right. It was then woven in two rows of pairing, starting about an inch from the center. A third row of pairing was then woven, dividing each group into groups of three each. The ends of the weavers were finished by cutting them at about an inch beyond the end of the third row of pairing and pushing each through a loop in the the weaving on the wrong side to hold it fast.

Each group of three spokes was then brought over the next group on the right, under the following one, over the next, under the next and outside (down by the weaving) making a loop about two and one half inches high, and leaving some long ends of each group. The first loops had to be left loose so the last two or three groups could be finished easily.

When this mat had been made even on all sides by pulling the loops out, and drawing them in, it was molded into a bowl shape with the hands. It was then placed, top downward, on the worker's knee, and a weaver of No. 2 rattan, doubled in the center, was started around the end of the group at the point on the circumference of the basket where the first pairing ended. Three rows of pairing were woven to make the beginning of a base, taking care not to draw in the group too much, but to keep the sides of the base straight. The end of each group was brought over the next group on the left, and pressed down inside the base, where it was cut off. The basket could then be finished with any of the polishes or finishes mentioned in the chapter on basket dyes or it could be left natural to age with time.

Modern makers of splint baskets are leaving them natural so they will age much more quickly, while the majority of pine needle basketmakers are now finishing their baskets with a solution of one-half denatured alcohol and one-half white shellac.

Possibly man watched birds weave their nests, thereby discovering the art of basketry. Once he had mastered the craft, and being an unselfish creature, man then wove nests for the birds. The first birds' nests were made of twigs and rush, and were sold at the bird market in Paris. Soon everyone was making birds' nests, including the children. The nests were kept dull and inconspicuous so the birds would accept them and nest in them.

The supply may soon have outnumbered the demand, although the nests are almost impossible to find today. Leaving them hanging in trees year after year took its toll. They were again so popular around the turn of the present century that most basket books carried instructions for at least one birds' nest.

In coiled baskets the weave or stitch was very important. In fact, the entire design depended upon it. Weaves listed in the books showing Indian basket weaving

Coiled-method stitching affects designs.

included Lazy Squaw, Mariposa, Toas, Samoan, and Klikitat.

In pine-needle basketry, today's makers have a choice of stitches. They can use Indian Squaw, chain, knot, popcorn, open V, diamond, Indian wrap, wheat, fern, or whirl. The skilled coil basketmakers insist that stitching requires concentration because the stitches must be consistent to obtain the best results. They also depend entirely on raffia today for the stitching because they say it should last about a hundred years, but many old pine needle baskets will still be found stitched with multicolored embroidery threads.

Only skilled basketmakers were able to make a perfect basket the first time they tried a new type. Sometimes they had to make several attempts before their work was correct. But no matter who made the basket, a few finishing touches always had to be made. The correct time for this was when the basket was first completed. Since it was still damp remedying irregularities in shape was simple. One side could even be a little higher than the other. It was easy to push one side down, or pull the other up before the material dried in place. After the basket dried, it was difficult or impossible to correct errors like flattening an uneven bottom. This applied only to the woven baskets since the coiled baskets were shaped as they were made. The maker had complete control over the shape because dried materials were used.

Whether the finished basket was perfect or filled with flaws, it reflected the individuality of the maker.

And for those who might still plan to become basketmakers, here are a few final tips. When work on the basket is completed, you will find there are some rough spots or hairlike fibers protruding here and there. Two of the best ways to solve these problems are either to singe the dry surface with the flame from a candle, being ever so careful not to scorch the surface, or to sand it thoroughly with fine sandpaper.

Side view of an open-work candy basket made by using the instructions given in this chapter. Only difference is that the maker used thirty-two pieces divided into groups of eight.

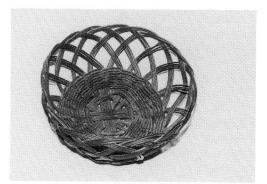

One type of candy basket base.

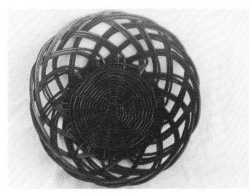

Another type base construction.

New pine needle basket showing raffia design in center.

Flared top willow basket showing construction.

Different design in new pine needle basket showing another base.

Rye basket.

Old pine needles stitched with embroidery thread.

5

Who Made It and What Was It For

The three questions most often asked about a basket are: Who made it? What was it made for? How old is it?

Something about any handmade items, especially baskets, just naturally brings out the first question. The item may be a hundred years old, and found in a deserted barn, but the first question that crosses the finder's mind is: I wonder who made this? We all have our own special fantasies of basketmakers, and they usually concern skillful little old ladies and gentlemen bent over a lapful of coils or splints, designing a basket that will be an absolute masterpiece—the one we have just found.

In reality it was the custom in many rural areas for the entire family to work most of the winter making baskets to sell the following spring and summer. It was a business—a sideline with many, it's true, but they treated it like a business most of the time.

There were those special occasions when these people wanted to make an unusual basket as a gift for a friend or family member, or even a special order for a customer willing to pay extra. Then there were those times when everything went exactly right and the basket being made was exceptionally pretty. The maker might decide to keep it for personal use.

In the spring the whole neighborhood might pool their baskets, allowing one or two persons to take a wagonload of them into the nearest town or city to be sold. Other than keeping each person's money separate so they could settle up when they got back home, there was little need for identification. The buyer, as a general rule, wasn't interested in who made the basket as long as it was attractive, well-made, and would serve its purpose. The seller didn't care because more like them would be made "come winter."

It is doubtful that either buyers or sellers, even in their wildest imaginings, ever dreamed that old baskets would be so popular, so high-priced, and so sought-after as they are now.

In some instances, the housewife found that certain makers produced a better basket than others, or at least one she thought was better and that fit her needs. Therefore she would wait until her favorite basketmaker came by with his wagonload of baskets.

Some of these baskets have been passed down through the family for several generations so the maker is well known. Each generation has told the next all about the maker of the treasured baskets. A few baskets have distinctive styles and can usually be identified by the advanced collector.

In some cases the basket might have been made by a member of the family, long since deceased, or it might have been bought or bartered from a special and well-known basketmaker. This doesn't happen often. But when its history and maker are known, the basket takes on new meaning and is more treasured. One example is a beautiful, carefully preserved, crossvine basket. Dated 1885, it was made by the present owner's great aunt.

One reason it is almost impossible to associate some of the old baskets with their former chores is that those chores no longer exist. Baskets shown in this old drawing were used in the silk mills around 1885 for sorting cocoons.

Old splint cotton basket with "hand holts" on either side.

The basketmakers may have had no specific purposes in mind for their products unless they were for their own personal use. In those days when there was little or no storage, a basket might be used for a dozen different chores in any one day.

A large number of baskets were made in a similar style for one particular purpose or chore for so long that they became known by that name. The so-called "egg basket" is an example. In the mountains of eastern Tennessee and Kentucky, in North Carolina, Virginia, and West Virginia, as well as portions of the border states, the gizzard-shaped or buttocks baskets were known far and wide as egg baskets. Over a long period of time the housewife used the basket for gathering eggs and taking them to the store either to be sold or bartered. Of course she might use an older, worn basket for gathering, and a pretty basket, maybe with a carved handle or fancy design, when going to the store. But they would still be called egg baskets.

In some other areas a basket with flat sides, apparently to fit snugly on the side of a horse's neck while transporting eggs to the nearby country store for trading, was also called an egg basket. Some of these baskets were made to hold exactly one dozen eggs without counting or breaking.

Like the egg basket, other baskets became known by the name of the job they were used for most often. In the Deep South a low, oblong splint basket was designed that was suitable to carry on an arm to gather the popular black-eyed or field peas. These baskets may not have been used too much during the past quarter century for pea picking, but to this day a basket of that general size and shape is known as a pea basket. Incidentally, these baskets did vary somewhat.

The pea harvest lasted only a couple of months at best. The pea baskets were used the balance of the year for other chores, from gathering corn to packing a picnic lunch for "All-Day Singing—Dinner on the Grounds" at the church. It didn't matter, they were still known as pea baskets.

The cotton basket has also retained its original name. Most cotton baskets were made with the materials on hand and the whims of the maker, but generally they are approximately twenty-five inches in both diameter and height. In some areas round baskets were more popular. In others the square or square-based ones were more frequently made. Again it probably depended upon the maker.

Square based cotton basket.

At one time, not so long ago, cotton was king in the South. It was THE money crop for farmers from Georgia to Texas, who grew it by the hundreds of acres. There were no mechanical cotton pickers at that time. The cotton had to be picked by hand, one boll at the time. The pickers went into the fields in droves, and they picked the long, white, fluffy cotton, putting it into cotton sacks they dragged behind them. When the sack was filled with cotton, the picker emptied it into the homemade, splint cotton baskets strategically located either at the end of the rows in small fields or in the middle of large ones.

At the end of the day all baskets of cotton were weighed so the pickers could be paid for their labors. Nobody ever weighed the baskets as it was an accepted fact that the basket weighed eight pounds, and that amount was deducted from the total weight of each basket of cotton before it was emptied into the wagons to be taken to the gin.

Alas, the days of the cotton basket were numbered. Soon cotton spreads of osnaburg would replace most of the baskets. The cotton baskets would hold less than a hundred pounds of packed cotton, but the cotton spread would hold two hundred pounds or more. A good cotton picker could pick two hundred pounds with ease, while a better than average picker could rack up four hundred pounds a day. The spreads were cheaper, more convenient, and easier to store when not in use, but they were not as useful around the farm as the old cotton baskets had been. For that reason cotton baskets continue to be used for other chores.

Just as the cotton spread had replaced the basket, the mechanical cotton picker replaced the spread. But before that happened, the boll weevil, an insect that came into the South and completely devoured the cotton bolls before they could mature, convinced Southern farmers to diversify. They began planting other crops, and cotton was no longer king. But the memory lives on. In the center of a small Southern town a monument to the boll weevil has been erected. And an ingenious basketmaker copied it in pine needle basketry.

Some of the gizzard-shaped or buttocks baskets never saw an egg. Instead they were used for a myriad of chores. They might be used to take seeds to the fields, or harvest the crop grown from those seeds. They might be used for storage of various items, or simply for holding "plunder," a word my grandmother used for everything that was left over, things you might eventually need, but that didn't fit any place else. Incidentally, she kept her plunder basket in the pantry.

The Indians originated the canoe-shaped basket, but the white man improved on the idea. It might not have been exactly an improvement, but he varied it so that it fit his needs better. Rather than make one long canoe-shaped basket as the Indians did, he made two ends, fastened them together so the open ends could be placed against his body at the waist, and with a thong around his neck to hold the basket, he had devised a "picking basket." Almost impossible to find now, they were excellent for picking apples, pears, peaches, and other fruit and berries.

The "clover basket" got its name because it was so closely woven it would hold any seed, even those as small as clover. Some baskets were named for the item they most closely resembled like the "watermelon," "muzzle," and "half-muzzle" baskets. Then there were others with strange-sounding names usually associated with their uses, like the quill basket. It was a flat, oval-shaped basket used long ago by loom weavers to hold quills for the shuttles.

Some baskets were named for the areas where they were first found like "Cobb County," "Old Kentucky," and "White Rock." The first square-end basket seen in one area came from the other side of the mountain, from a place called White Rock, hence the name. There are also baskets known as "jug baskets," and it is not known how or where they got the name unless they were used to carry or store a jug of homemade corn whiskey.

It is not unusual to see photos or etchings from Ireland, Scotland, and Jamaica of the natives carrying a melon basket. In the mountains they were called "hip baskets."

It is entirely possible many of the baskets attributed to the Western Indians were actually made by housewives all over the country. During the early part of this century advertisements in numerous magazines ran over a long period of time, offering to send not only instructions, but also a "commenced basket."

The following advertisement appeared repeatedly in numerous magazines during 1902: "Indian Basketry – Taught by Mail – Easily learned by Anyone – A Popular and Lucrative Pastime – Special outfit consists of commenced basket of genuine Navajo weave – enough material to complete it – needle, working plan, and instructions prepaid for $1.00 (no stamps or personal checks) – Booklet of prices of material and designs sent with each order or for 4 cents postage." It could be ordered from the Navajo School of Indian Basketry, California.

Hickey-made basket.

The history of the so-called "Hickey baskets," named for their maker, is also known. The owner of one of these baskets passed down through the family says her grandmother bought baskets from an Indian man named Hickey. He used to travel through sections of eastern Tennessee (perhaps other areas also) during the early 1900s.

Going from farmhouse to farmhouse and possibly into towns and cities, Hickey traded his handmade willow baskets for eggs, chickens, vegetables, or other food items. No doubt there were instances when he sold his baskets for cash, but he is best remembered for his bartering. In his territory he became a popular man because the people liked his baskets. Housewives in need of new baskets looked forward to his spring arrival. Some even sent word ahead to neighbors he might call on first to tell Hickey they needed baskets right away.

Although not plentiful, Hickey's baskets still turn up in the areas where he worked. It is easy to identify them even now since they are all basically made alike (sizes and shapes may vary) with a handle that seems to have been his trademark. To have had enough baskets to tour the country each spring, it is possible Hickey's family also made baskets.

Well over half a century has passed since Hickey stopped traveling around the country selling his baskets. But he is remembered as kindly today by the people who own examples of his work and display it proudly as he was by the housewives who bought his baskets many years ago.

In later years the barter system diminished into whatever price a basket would bring. But in the early years in the mountains there was a strict basket-bartering code. Prices, or the equivalent, were fixed according to size. When trading, it was the custom to allow the basketmaker as much corn as the basket would hold. In other words, for a peck basket, he received a peck of corn, or whatever was being traded. For a bushel basket, he received a bushel of corn. This method doesn't seem quite fair because as much work, maybe more, was required to make a small basket as a large one. But in those days all types of labor were a cheap commodity.

Seeing the special care and consideration given the baskets whose makers are known makes you realize that the history of the basket and identification of the maker is important. Unfortunately, most records of makers have been lost, if they were known in the first place. For that reason, those who have a basket whose history is known should list it and attach it to the basket for future generations.

Among the many uses the early settlers found for their baskets is one that may experience a revival now that growing your own herbs is again becoming so popular. The basket is used for gathering herbs, letting some types dry in the baskets. In those early days they used whatever basket was handy. It might be the old egg basket or a pea basket. But it has been found that baskets with low sides actually work better unless a person is gathering many small herbs. Then the deeper basket is better. Today the trend is to gather the herbs in the low round baskets, the ones that were used so much in the twenties and thirties for gathering cut flowers. Now these baskets are as popular as ever since they can be used for both flower and herb gathering.

Standard style for Hickey. Note identical handle construction.

Note similarity to other Hickey-made baskets.

Size is different and handle lower, but definitely a Hickey basket.

When traveling, short trips or long ones, ladies took along a basket. It might contain food or their most precious possession.

Small harvesting basket on the cotton-basket style.

It was the custom for a lady to take her basket when she went to visit a neighbor or just for a stroll.

Larger harvesting basket.

Originally this was probably a picking basket of some kind. Now it makes an excellent display for old keys.

Fancy pea basket.

Taller handle and flared top, but still a Hickey-made basket.

Well-worn pea basket.

Pea basket made for service, not beauty.

Plain pea basket.

Only the maker knows what this basket was made for originally.

Basket with one handle and sloping side apparently for pouring out contents, probably apples or other fruit. Raised center indicates it was made for a more delicate fruit, one that would be crushed by too much weight in the center.

Oblong, flat-bottom, splint basket.

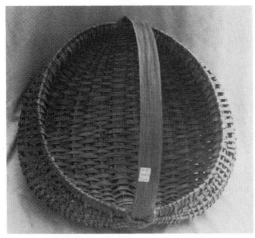

Perfect example of the gizzard-shaped or buttocks basket. Called an egg basket in some areas.

Sometimes baskets are kept for sentimental reasons. The owner of this one carried it filled with flowers when she served as bridesmaid at her best friend's wedding in 1920.

Worn example of old egg basket. Worn ones are cheaper than the perfect ones.

Serviceable egg basket.

Two sizes of egg baskets.

Another style egg basket.

Four styles of baskets with eggs in square one.

Collection of various style baskets.

Painted splint egg basket.

At an antique show, eggs were shown in this style basket.

Melon-shaped baskets are often called egg baskets in some areas.

Basket was worn on the back to carry wood for the fires.

Large melon-shaped basket used for a variety of chores.

Original use for this oblong basket with shaped handle is unknown.

Gizzard or buttocks baskets in four sizes.

Basket still holds "plunder."

Large, deep, square splint basket.

Known primarily as a laundry basket, it was also used for harvesting. The housewife used this type basket for a baby bed when she had to go to the fields or travel in the wagon.

Wide-splint laundry basket.

New England style basket.

Shallow tray-type basket could be used for many chores.

Owner of this basket took pies and cakes to church socials in it.

This basket was aged naturally and is now used for gathering cut flowers and herbs.

Same type basket painted white.

Hanging basket is excellent for growing herbs in the kitchen.

Basket holds wildflower blossoms cut for drying.

Discarded fishing creel makes excellent kitchen planter for herbs.

56

Old splint basket, well-lined to prevent moisture from seeping through, also makes excellent herb planter.

⁖ 6 ⁖

Oriental Baskets

Like everything else in the antiques and collectibles field, some baskets are sought after, with collectors paying unbelievable prices for them. Other baskets go begging for a buyer at nearly any price, but usually one ridiculously low, considering they are all handmade. This is the story today of the Cinderella of antique baskets, the American handmade splints, and fancy Western Indian baskets versus the evil stepmother of the basket world, the Oriental baskets.

Perhaps part of this stems from the fact that Americans are intrigued with Country Americana objects. They also remember the stories told about the native-made baskets and basketmakers. Therefore they think of them as a part of their history. The Oriental baskets were made "across the waters" as one old-timer explained, and they had never been used or enjoyed like the native-made baskets.

Oriental baskets were distinct from those made in the United States. The materials used in construction were different, and the Oriental baskets were sold in the "dime stores," not by your neighbor or someone you knew. The finer Oriental baskets were sold in gift shops, but the majority of people who bought, made, and used splint or coiled baskets were not frequent shoppers in the better gift shops.

Oriental baskets are still the best buys on the market, if you like the type, and some gorgeous ones are available. These baskets were made by hand as were the splints and coils made in this country. The workmanship is as good, sometimes better, and the designs as varied and ornate. Oriental baskets are as old, often older, than many of the baskets locally made. Yet they are not priced nearly as high—

A Formosan basket made around 1900. Area is now Taiwan and is still noted for excellent basketry.

sometimes less than one-fourth the price—as the splints. Even so, they still sell much more slowly. Possibly collectors don't like the materials—most often bamboo—used to make them.

The quality of the workmanship in Oriental baskets is excellent. The Japanese took great pride in their basketry. It was back in 1911 that one writer described their work this way: "Many of the native specimens [baskets], excellent as they are artistically, are not made as works of art at all, but as objects of utility—such as fish baskets and sieves, and the worker merely introduced the artistic element as the work proceeded."

That is the biggest advantage of making anything by hand; the talented worker can improvise as the work progresses.

It has been noted throughout the years that the Japanese and Chinese, thinking the Americans wanted it that way, have made a much more elaborate specimen for export. Ornately carved teakwood is an example. For their own uses they kept the plainer, less heavily carved pieces. Unlike the other items, it appears most of the exported baskets were similiar to the ones they kept for their own needs. But uses for the baskets varied from country to country.

Many of the American and European-made baskets have similarities about them, but the Oriental examples seem to vary considerably. Both the Japanese and Chinese were liberally endowed with patience and artistic talents, so it would only be natural that they would design and make extraordinary baskets.

Turn-of-the-century visitors to Japan were duly impressed by the daintiness of all their baskets. At that time, basket-makers set up shop on the streets, others took baskets in pushcarts and plied their trade wherever customers could be found. One visitor later wrote that he was very much impressed by the dainty baskets used by the fruit merchants to display their wares in the railroad stations.

One Japanese writer of that period expressed the wish that visitors to his country would take time "to notice the very important part that bamboo baskets played in general usefulness as well as in decorations."

Baskets for the most humble chores received the same attention and were made of the same materials as those that would be used for the most prestigious. As much artistic skill was utilized to make a salt basket that would be nailed to the kitchen wall as was used to make the finest flower basket.

In the early Japanese homes a brazier was used to heat each room. The sumitori-kago (basket) used for holding the brazier charcoal was a necessary item, yet it was

In Japan they were called basket weavers. Old photo shows them working in their shop.

Japanese basket seller with load of newly made baskets on his two-wheel cart (from old photo).

not on display, but kept discreetly pushed away in the corner. The makers of these baskets knew they would seldom if ever be seen, yet they made them in a variety of shapes and styles. Even in these baskets workmanship was excellent, and all had delicate finishes.

Japan has long been known as a leader in arranging both fresh and artificial flowers. Naturally they found their locally made baskets were the best containers for flowers, possibly the only decorative containers. It seems that each complemented the other. Known as hana-kago, these flower baskets were used either for ikebana flower arranging or for the zokwa (to decorate with artificial flowers).

The baskets usually contained a piece of whole bamboo with a joint at the bottom so it would hold water. Later versions were fitted with either the bamboo or a zinc or copper tube. The most popular flowers for use in the hana-kago were irises or chrysanthemums, depending upon the season. It was said that a few of either flower arranged in a basket with an enormous bamboo handle gave the impression of a halo around the flowers.

Nearly a century ago the custom of exchanging gifts for no apparent reason seemed to flourish in Japan. One of the most commonly given gifts was a mori-kago (fruit basket) filled with in-season fruit. Often the mori-kago was more valuable than the contents.

Bamboo basketry was also used to make handbags of all shapes and sizes, as well as cigar and cigarette cases, tobacco pouches, lunch boxes, and some of the tiny baskets used in the doll festivals. The Chinese made the same type items, but added a special touch on some of their handbags—a puzzle fastener.

Bamboo was by no means the only material used to make baskets in China and Japan. Other commonly used substances were rattan, vines, and willow. Around 1908, hundreds of acres of unused castle grounds all over Japan were planted with young willow trees. The reasons were partly to provide materials for baskets and wicker furniture, and partly to utilize the idle land. Experts say that by using the best methods, a willow bed can be in full production within three years, and will continue to produce for another ten years.

Both the Chinese and Japanese are noted for the rich brown color of their best old bamboo baskets. This did not occur by accident, nor was it achieved with dyes—a method used later. Early on it was a planned operation. To make the much sought after, mellow brown baskets, it was customary for the makers to search out bamboo pieces from old homes—ones that age and smoke from many fires had tinted to just the right shade.

Now, so many years later, it would be almost impossible for an American collector to determine which baskets were made by the leading makers of that period without going to Japan and thoroughly researching the subject. There is also the possibility that much of the history of the baskets and the old basketmakers has been destroyed. But hopefully the Japanese have retained as much or more than we have.

The best known and most distinguished of the early 1900 Japanese basketmakers were Iizuka Hosia of Tokyo, Morita Skintaro of Kyoto, and Ogawa Nihei who was living and working in Osaka. Much of the best bamboo came from the vicinity of Kyoto, which was famous for growing a tall, strong strain, and the city of Shidzuoka was probably the most famous for having an abundance of good basketmakers.

Oriental bamboo basket.

Listed as a Japanese egg basket, it bears no resemblance to an American egg basket.

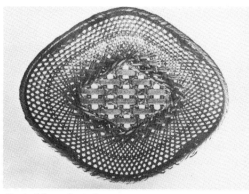

Probably a fruit basket.

Inexpensive bamboo baskets like this were plentiful in the United States fifty years ago.

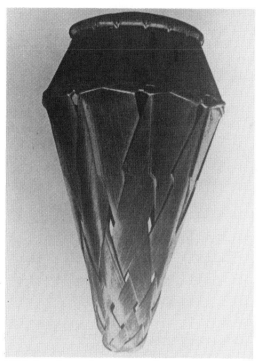

Wide bamboo strips were used to make this hanging flower basket.

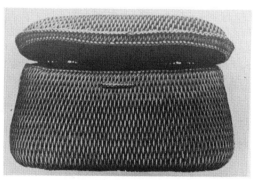

A Japanese tobacco pouch.

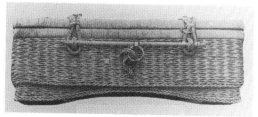

In Japan this was called a lunch basket.

Basket made with dark, aged bamboo.

In America they were called vases, in Japan flower baskets.

Bamboo flower basket.

Tall-handled, bamboo flower basket.

Small, Oriental novelty basket.

Three small novelty baskets from the Orient.

Mothers often lined the small, inexpensive Oriental baskets to hold dolls.

Vine basket of Oriental origin.

Hexagonal, openwork weaves were popular with both Japanese and American basketmakers.

Two small imported baskets believed to be made of some type of paper, probably rice paper.

7

May Baskets

The origin of the custom of giving May baskets, small baskets filled with spring flowers, to friends seems to be lost somewhere in the mists of antiquity, but it is believed to have developed from an old English custom. For fifty years or longer it was the custom in some areas of the United States for children to take small baskets of flowers to elderly people and shut-ins as well as anyone they wanted to remember on the first day of May.

Although some grown-ups delivered May baskets, it was generally the children who looked forward to that day the most. It was an opportunity to repay someone for a small kindness. Seldom were the flowers purchased. Instead they were gathered from the family garden or nearby fields and meadows. They might be wildflowers, or some of the finest in the garden. It wasn't the flower that counted as much as the thought.

This seemed to be one of the more subtle, yet simple, ways parents of long ago used to teach their children the joy of giving and sharing.

For several decades around the turn of the present century (as late as the 1930s) young girls hoarded every small basket they could find during the year. They were stored carefully to await the coming May. In most rural areas, small baskets of the type merchants gave away, weren't plentiful. The small four-inch by six-inch, factory-made splints were the cheapest and easiest to find, and the ones most commonly used for May baskets. Depending upon the area, these little baskets came filled with candy, mushrooms, or kumquats. In the South, little girls begged for kumquats so they could have the baskets.

May basket filled with wisteria, dogwood, and honeysuckle blossoms as it might have been half a century ago.

Other sources included the local merchant or owner of the crossroads general store. They were asked to save all the small baskets, including the damaged ones, that would otherwise have been thrown away. Damaged places in the baskets would not show when filled with flowers.

The baskets might not have been as plentiful as the little girls would have liked, but May Day morning was a happy time for all of them. The baskets had been brought out the night before and cleaned in anticipation of the big event. In some areas the baskets might even have been painted or decorated. It all depended upon the time and talents of the mother—whether or not she worked with her children.

The baskets were all waiting, so early in the morning the girls gathered the flowers they had been watching for weeks, hoping they would be in full bloom at just the right time. The flowers would be placed in the baskets, and the girls would start on their rounds. They would go from house to house delivering the baskets of flowers and visiting with the family for a few minutes.

It is thought this practice could have been derived from the Old English custom of "going a-Maying." During the sixteenth and seventeenth centuries it was customary for the people of the middle and lower classes in England to go out very early on the first day of May to gather flowers and hawthorn branches. Accompanied by the music of a horn and tabor and much laughter and merriment, the people returned home with their flowers and branches about sunrise. They then began to decorate the doors and windows of all the houses in their village. By natural transition they gave the name May to the hawthorn blossom, hence the expression "the bringing home the May."

In earlier times, the celebration had been more popular and had been attended by royalty as well as the middle and lower classes. In those times the upper classes joined in the fun. In fact, there was a time when the kings and queens condescended to mingle with their subjects on May Day.

One recorded event of this occasion occurred during the reign of Henry VIII when someone wrote:

"The heads of the corporations of London went out into the high grounds of Kent to gather the May, the king and his queen, Catherine of Aragon, coming from their palace at Greenwich, and met these respected dignitaries on Shooter's Hill."

May Day activities were celebrated throughout the British Empire and were noted by several writers of importance. Chaucer in his *Court of Love* refers to May Day as the time when "Forth goeth all the court, both most and least, to fetch the flowers fresh," while in *Shepherd's Calendar* we read:

"Of lonely nymphs – Oh that I were
   there
To help the ladies their May-bush to
   bear!"

So May Day, as the first day of the fifth month, had become so commonly known that it has long been an important day in the lives of the English-speaking people. One reason could have been that they were certain that spring had arrived and were happy it was time to get out of the house— shed the cloak of winter. After some of the long, cold winters they experienced, warm days were more than enough cause for celebration.

Those tiny baskets of flowers delivered by young twentieth-century maidens were the dying embers of a custom that had begun many centuries before. It is rare when the mention of May baskets is now heard, indicating that this custom, like going a-Maying, is passing into oblivion.

8

Sewing Baskets

Centuries ago only the monks in the monasteries and nuns in the convents did fancy stitchery. No doubt they also did some simple stitchery as they, like everyone else, had to have clothing of some kind. Then there were seamstresses who made clothing for the general public, the ones who could afford the better clothing. Ready-made clothing was unknown at that time. Undoubtedly someone did darning and mending then, but it was such a common chore that history failed to record it.

Fancy stitchery records are almost as skimpy, but they do credit the monks and nuns with developing fancy stitchery such as embroidery and lacemaking. Centuries later knitting, crocheting, and tatting would be developed. In time the nuns and monks began teaching the inhabitants of their villages to do fancy stitchery, and they in turn taught others. Once they had learned the many ways they could use a needle and thread they not only did fancy stitchery but also plain sewing as well. And they must have learned patching and darning early because clothing was scarce in those days.

Hand sewing was the only kind known at that time, since the sewing machine was not developed until well into the 1800s. Even the ladies on the *Mayflower,* awaiting the building of homes in the New World, spent much of their time either doing some type of needlework or teaching their daughters beginning stitches so they could make samplers.

Once they were settled in their new homes, which might have been only single-room log cabins, they were responsible for weaving fabrics for both the family clothing and household linens. In those days household linens were not plentiful. In fact they were so scarce and so treasured that some wills dated in the 1600s listed household linens. One of the favorites was the "cubberd cloth" thought to be a cloth for a cupboard.

Producing the fabric for the cubberd cloth or for clothing in those days meant starting from scratch. The workers had to shear the sheep, clean, dye, and spin the wool into thread, and then weave it into fabric. Later there would be flax for making linen or for mixing with wool to make linsey-woolsey. Preparing either for weaving was a time-consuming chore. Everything about the lives of these early settlers was time-consuming, from washing the clothes in the nearby creek to cooking food all day on an open fire. Their time had to be budgeted with just so many hours to spend on spinning and weaving. Therefore these people had to make each garment last as long as possible.

They considered themselves lucky if they had two outfits at one time, one to wear around the house, the other to be worn to church and funerals. Naturally, they weren't about to throw away a garment just because of a small rip or even a worn place. If patching and darning hadn't been learned earlier, the women learned fast in the New World. In the early days it was easy to keep some thread from the original fabric for mending or patching, but as time passed matching the old fabric did become a problem.

As these struggling citizens of the New World became more affluent, they acquired a few labor-saving devices. For the less fortunate it might have been a roasting jack for cooking meat or an oven built in the side of the fireplace for baking bread. The rich planters and merchants acquired servants. They might be slaves or paid servants, but with the extra help the housewife was able to do more weaving or have the servants do it.

Along with the luxury of more clothing and household linens, came the responsibility of more upkeep such as mending. So now enough thread from each dye lot had to be kept to repair the garments made from it. It is difficult today to control the exact color of each dye lot. However, back in those days it was even harder as the threads were dyed under primitive conditions and by primitive methods.

In those early days there wasn't a pressing need for storage space. Families had little to store. But as the number of their possessions increased so did their need for storage. Baskets were used for many storage needs including sewing items like thread, needles, thimbles, and scissors. In the early days any type basket was used for sewing. It might be an oak splint with or without a handle, or it might be one made of willow or vines. Regardless, the basket was used to keep all milady's sewing needs together so she could take her basket with her at night when she sat down either to mend or do some kind of fancy needlework.

Many possibilities for convenient storage of sewing items were explored, such as sewing bags and sewing tables, and later wicker sewing stands. Regardless of what else they might acquire, most ladies still clung to their small sewing basket, one that would fit into her lap or on the table beside her. Some of the choicest sewing tools like the silver tatting shuttles, gold and silver thimbles, scissors, stilettos, and sterling-handled darning eggs have been found in those old baskets.

Sewing baskets were so common that records of them or their use were not kept. But somewhere around the turn of the twentieth century the Chinese and Japanese realized what an extensive market for sewing baskets existed in America. They began making and exporting them by boatloads. This practice was continued well into the 1930s.

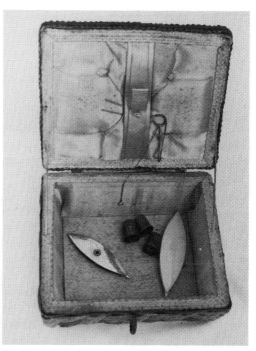

Inside of basket with thimbles and tatting shuttles.

Sweet grass holder for thimble.

Most Oriental sewing baskets were made of bamboo, either very wide or very naroow strips, or a combination of the two. Some were reasonably plain, but the majority were fancy. Some were open and fitted with small, doll-like figures and sewing tools. Others had covers decorated with coins from the country of origin along with beads and tassels. And then there were some baskets probably not intended to be sewing baskets. But these appealed to their owners who made them into sewing baskets.

Owner remembers grandmother using this one as sewing basket.

The Oriental baskets were much lighter in weight than the old woven splint or willow baskets, which made them seem less strong, but they lasted well. Colorful and different from locally made baskets, Oriental baskets were attractive to the ladies—and they were inexpensive. These baskets could usually be bought for ten cents to seldom over twenty-five cents. Exclusive gift shops offered fitted sewing baskets, some with sterling silver sewing tools.

All baskets were inexpensive in those days, so at those prices the ladies felt no qualms about discarding an old sewing basket whenever a new style or design caught their eye. This was also a time of gift giving, and what would make a nicer gift than a sewing basket, since every woman needed or could use a new sewing basket.

Basket factories started up all over America. The big difference in baskets now was that American baskets were machine made, while Oriental baskets were still handmade. No doubt this difference was noted by the ladies. Recognizing the appeal of the imported sewing baskets to the women, the American basketmakers began producing similar items. However, the materials used here were not the same. Generally they were made of sweet grasses and raffia and had hinged covers. Later they would be made of fiber rush, a type of twisted paper developed to replace the willow and reed used to make wicker furniture. The American-made sewing baskets had a hinged lid—a decided advantage because it prevented the lid from being misplaced. Many of the baskets had satin linings, which gave them a luxurious appearance that appealed to a luxury-hungry public.

Some of the baskets were also fitted and a bit more expensive, but it didn't seem to hinder sales. Judging by the baskets available today, it would seem that the ordinary sweet grass sewing baskets with satin linings were about as popular as the round bamboo examples. Both can still be found in antique shows, shops, malls, and flea markets. Prices remain modest, and once in a great while a basket will be found with sewing tools intact.

Footed bamboo sewing basket.

Plain bamboo sewing basket.

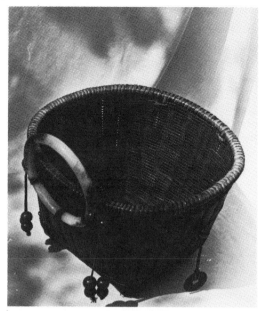

Open bamboo basket used for sewing.

Open, fitted sewing basket.

Sweet grass sewing basket.

Willow basket also used as sewing basket.

Fiber rush sewing basket.

❖ 9 ❖

Decorating with Baskets

At one time collectors assembled large numbers of old baskets with no thought of ever using them, only possessing them and perhaps displaying a few. But things have changed drastically in the past few years. Now collectors who are afraid of harming their expensive old baskets buy new ones to use—the handmade ones that show up at arts and crafts shows. There seems to be a trend across the country today to use your baskets, and use them, we do.

New uses are appearing every day. Some innovative ideas not only show off the baskets but also whatever they contain for display, from fruit and nuts to potted plants or cut flowers.

Time was when a collection of baskets was displayed in a conglomeration, if it was shown at all. This could have been an assemblage of the baskets on an old hall tree, the four-sided post variety. Dowels could be placed at intervals along the post on which the baskets would be hung. Or the baskets could have been strung on a rope at intervals, and hung in the corner of a room or on a porch. Another favorite spot for displaying baskets was on the top of kitchen wall cabinets, near the ceiling. In country kitchens, the baskets might have been displayed in open cabinets.

Another way to exhibit a collection of good, old baskets, still used frequently today, is to hang them from the beams in either the kitchen or game room.

Most baskets are all nearly the same color—unless they have been dyed. So there is a sameness about them when they are all displayed together. They need the addition of something colorful. Old baskets

Collection of baskets displayed on converted hat rack.

are especially attractive if copper or brass pieces are used with them. Blue and white graniteware mixed with the baskets adds charm.

Of course, with unusually large collections, displaying them can pose a problem. One collector found that she had a change of scenery as well as feeling that her rooms had been redecorated when she displayed about half her collection for six months, then packed it away and displayed the other half.

There are numerous ways to display a basket collection, but perhaps none is as effective as using the baskets. When used for any of the many purposes collectors are finding today, their beauty is more pronounced.

Baskets filled with dried flowers are popular. Some of these arrangements are so beautiful they fit nicely with formal furniture. The baskets, because of their various styles and designs, lend themselves to many different flowers and foliage. Tall arrangements fit well into the deeper baskets, and short-stemmed ones fit the smaller baskets.

Baskets holding arrangements of artificial fruits and flowers look decorative. An illustration in this chapter shows a later, well-worn basket filled with discarded artificial fruit. The entire arrangement was painted white and hung on the front door for the holidays. It was then packed away until the following Christmas, when it was brought out, painted gold, and again hung on the door.

Within the last few years, various basket arrangements have decorated the front door or a space beside the door year-round. Those who hesitate to leave their expensive old baskets outside for long periods of time are now using newer baskets or basketry items for this purpose.

Christmas seems to be the time to use baskets to greater advantage. Old, worn baskets can be painted red or green and filled with Christmas greenery. Candy canes add to the arrangement and to the color. Again, if the owner prefers not to use an old basket, new ones will work equally well. In fact, they are very attractive left natural. Good baskets should not be painted unless they were bought specifically for that purpose. Paint won't harm damaged baskets, which can often be bought much cheaper than newer ones. Since the baskets will be used for only a short time, and paint covers much of the damage, they can be most attractive.

During the holiday season baskets filled with Christmas tree balls make lovely centerpieces. Satin balls decorated with old lace and beads make a special kind of decoration, and a personal one that ties in with

Damaged basket and discarded fruit painted white.

Damaged basket painted red, and filled with holly and candy canes.

New basket filled with greenery and candy canes.

other antiques. These arrangements can be used on tables in small apartments in place of a Christmas tree when space is a problem.

An old cotton basket is useful for holding logs by the fireplace. A basket generally used to gather flowers can hold magazines or small logs. Large pine cones in a basket look especially attractive near a fireplace.

Small baskets of tiny cones or burrs make an unusual centerpiece for bridge or party tables during the autumn. In fact, baskets can be used year-round to show off what nature has provided. Beginning in early spring there are wild flowers or garden flowers, then the summer fruits and vegetables. And nothing shows off brilliantly colored fruits and vegetables like an old basket. In the fall colorful foliage along with the season's vegetables and fruits are eyecatching. Or you might prefer a few branches of ripe persimmons mixed with the leaves. When these disappear the Christmas season is upon us, and the uses for baskets are limitless.

Baskets make unique holders for wooden cooking tools. They are not only an attractive way to use smaller baskets, but they also add a homey touch to any country kitchen. For color you may want to add a few pretty quilted pot holders or a kitchen towel or two.

Just as in grandma's day, baskets make excellent storage or holders for colorful guest towels. On top of the cabinet, they will look pretty and be easy for guests to find.

The old baskets with flat sides, made in a variety of styles, can be used in many different ways. Holding a Christmas arrangement on the front door is probably the first one that comes to mind, but they can be used in any room in the house. Hung on the bathroon wall, these baskets can hold towels. In the kitchen they can hold tools. A small basket filled with artificial flowers and hung on the bathroom wall is especially pretty when color-coordinated with the towels. You could pair small pink

Pine cones in splint basket.

Tiny burrs and cones in small basket.

roses with pink towels; blue morning glories with blue towels; and purple violets, either fresh or artificial, with lavender towels.

Fresh flowers are as easy to display in baskets as the artificial. Only a small tin or glass container is necessary. Simply insert it in the basket to hold water for the flowers.

Baskets are being used more and more to hold live potted plants. Again, precautions must be taken to prevent surplus water from ruining the basket. A plastic or a glass container can be put in the basket under the pot holding the plant. Or the plant can be taken out of the basket to be watered. The smaller baskets make excellent holders for gaily blooming plants, and the newer, less expensive basket filled with a blooming, potted plant makes a memorable gift.

The old, open-work candy baskets and bread baskets make useful holders for knitting, crocheting, or needlepoint yarns.

Artificial eggs and berries in new basket.

Dried arrangement in willow twig basket.

Low arrangement in high-handled Oriental basket.

Colorful yarns and maybe a pair of old wooden knitting needles or crochet hooks add to the decor of a room furnished with antiques.

There is an added bonus for those who have pieces of yarn left over from needlework and crafts. With a blunt needle threaded with the surplus yarn make attractive designs on the newer, less expensive baskets—the ones found at flea markets for a dollar or two. Add a few old beads or small artificial flowers to create your own design and color scheme.

Apples in flat basket.

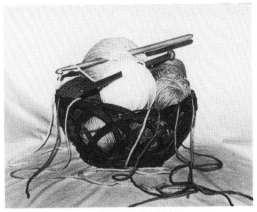

Balls of yarn in open basket.

Flowers and yarn design added to late, inexpensive basket.

❖ 10 ❖

Novelties and Miniatures in Basketry

Any craftsman worth his salt is going to experiment. As soon as he learns the basics of his craft and is able to make a variety of accepted items, he or she will begin to experiment—just to see what can be made. This is as true of furniture making as painting, and it spills over into basketry. In fact, basketry is one craft that lends itself well to novelties and miniatures. It has always been used to make small trinkets. Sometimes they were necessary; sometimes just decorative, but all are interesting nevertheless.

Some of the earliest basket items that would be classified now as novelties were made by the Indians. They used willow to make a doll bed, called a cradle by early researchers, but an item that more closely resembled the carriers mothers used to transport babies on their backs. They also made a fabric-bodied doll with a wooden head to be placed in the bed or cradle. No doubt they made other toys and novelties for their children as well as themselves, but records are skimpy.

Another Indian-made item that would probably be classified as a novelty today, but necessary for the Indians, was the ha-kin-ne, a sort of ring-shaped pad made of woven yucca leaves. It was made and used mostly by the Zuni, but could have been used by others as well. One side of the pad was made to fit the top of the wearer's head, while the other fit the water jug or bowl. This container was used to carry water from the nearest stream. The original idea, no doubt, was to make something

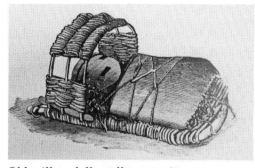

Old willow doll cradle or carrier.

Indian ha-kin-ne was used to carry water on the head.

that would take some of the pressure of the water jug off the wearer's head. But it was soon found that the ha-kin-ne helped to balance the container as the person walked so it ended up serving a dual role.

The pioneers used willow and a couple of acorns to make a toy rattle for their children. They also used basketry to make essential things like ox muzzles, eel traps, and apple-drying baskets—things we would probably consider novelties today.

Then there were the basketmakers who just wanted to see what they could concoct from materials on hand, or left over from a regular basket project. These artful expressions became the miniatures and novelties that excite collectors today. They are scarce. But every collector has at least one special miniature or novelty mixed in with other baskets.

It seems that with each basket revival there comes a new wave of miniatures and novelties. Like the Indian doll carrier and the pioneer baby rattle, there might have been a need or a use for it. In other cases it was made to test the skill of the maker.

Until the current renewed interest in baskets, the last really substantial revival occurred around the turn of the present century. At that time, books, pamphlets, and advertisements in leading magazines not only encouraged the housewife to start making baskets, but also tried to entice the whole family. Occasionally a basket novelty would be mentioned, but the majority of them have been made by some basketmaker who was either trying to make something needed or something like the coiled, pine-needle cup and saucer. A novelty like this could be shown off on the Victorian whatnot without being obvious. Middle-class Victorian etiquette demanded that you never praise your own work or that of some member of your family. It was not only acceptable but permissible to use every trick in the book to get others to praise your work.

The beaches were not as accessible then as now. In fact, there weren't even roads to many of them located away from large cities. Unless you lived within a few hundred miles of a beach you didn't go at all. Beach visitors spent much of their time picking up shells. Once they were home again, they tried to use the shells in any craft they were involved in at the time. If they could incorporate the shell in some of their handicrafts, it would be so much easier to show it off. Therefore, they would not break all the rules by bragging that they were at the beach three summers ago. A favorite way to use seashells was for decorating a tray. The bottom could be filled with the seashells in an artistic design. The sides could be made of coiled pine needles. These trays were especially popular in the South, where both shells and pine needles were plentiful. The trays can still be found in many estate sales.

Another still-popular phase of basketry is the miniature basket. Many basketmakers work long hours to make the tiny baskets. A photograph at the end of this chapter shows two of these baskets with a dime and will give you an idea of how small they actually are. The larger one measures one inch across the top, and is one and three-eighths inch from the bottom to the top of the handle. The smaller one is approximately five-eights inch in diameter and one and one-fourth inches from the bottom to the top of the handle.

It is extremely difficult and time-consuming to make baskets with splints cut almost as fine as thread. But some basketmakers still make a few of these. One problem is cutting the splints fine enough without cutting through them. Exceptionally good eyesight and patience are required both to cut the splints and to weave the baskets.

About a decade or so ago a basketmaker's husband was at a flea market, and around his neck was a necklace made of dozens of tiny gizzard-shaped or buttocks baskets. The baskets were barely an inch in diameter and the splints were almost as fine as sewing thread. They were exquisite.

Old-timers were apt to make a novelty like a pitcher, knowing it would serve no purpose other than decorative. The makers gave little or no thought to these items being useful and were simply proving a point—they could adapt basketry to any shape or form.

Hanging wall cases, treasured now, if they can be found, were also made. Likely they were designed to hold combs, but it is possible they were also used in other ways. In those days comb cases were made in a variety of materials, but the woven splint examples are extremely scarce today.

A doll sofa made of woven splints is a related item. The owner did a tremendous amount of research before he discovered the original purpose. He has been unable to obtain the matching chair. It is possible these sets were made in only one section of the country, and perhaps by only one maker. Scarcity would almost bear this out.

Coiled, rye beehives were not a novelty then, nor are they novelties today. They are scarce and very collectible. Nothing rounds out a basket collection like a dozen examples of coiled, rye basketry that includes a beehive. Perhaps it is the novel idea rather than the novelty that makes them so desirable.

Not an antique, but desirable collectibles are ladies' purses made in the style of the Nantucket lightship baskets. The old and very desirable Nantucket lightship baskets were made by the sailors stationed on the lightship outside Nantucket harbor around the middle to late 1800s. This had been a famous whaling area, but after the discovery of petroleum, or kerosene, for the lamps, whale oil was no longer essential. Whaling all but ceased. A lighthouse was needed at this point, but it would have been impossible to build one there, so a lightship was anchored instead. The sailors had little to do except to keep the lights burning, so they made baskets—in a distinctive style— to pass the time. These baskets are now so scarce and so expensive they are seldom included in basketry books. Collectors know what they are, and others have little or no interest in them.

In the 1940s a Filipino gentleman began making a basket with a lid, using the style and weave of the old Nantucket lightship baskets. Others joined him. Unfortunately, his basket purses are not as famous nor as sought-after as the baskets they were copied from, but they are well worth collecting. A decided advantage to the purses is that many have the initials or name of the maker either on the bottom or on a small disc on the lid. Of course, given time, these may become as sought-after as the original Nantucket lightship baskets.

The son of another skilled basketmaker challenged his mother to make him a cowboy hat, using only pine needles. She spent weeks just trying to figure out how to start, but once she began it was down hill the rest of the way. She spent four months making it, and says now the most difficult part was shaping it.

It is neither a miniature nor a novelty. Perhaps oddity would be a better word to describe the excellent quality old leather-bound fishing creels that are showing up in some of the better antique shops these days. They are also being included in some basket collections, probably to show the scope of basketry. No use other than decorative has been found so far unless, like the later, cheaper fishing creels, damaged ones might be used for flower arrangements or for plants.

Old tray made of pine needles and seashells.

Old pine needle cup and saucer novelty.

Miniature baskets shown with a dime.

Old wall hanging case, probably a comb case.

Old woven splint pitcher.

Owner calls this a doll sofa.

Old rye beehive.

Small new baskets made with finely cut splints.

New pine needle cowboy hat.

Replica of the boll weevil made of pine needles.

Late lady's purse made after the style of the Nantucket lightship baskets.

Old leather-bound fishing creel.

11

Food and Beverage Basketry

The gathering of eggs and peas was not the only time baskets were closely associated with food products. Looking back, baskets were used for everything from planting through harvesting and on to storing the foods whenever necessary. And the use of baskets didn't stop there. Prepared foods were taken to church dinners and picnics—oftentimes in the same baskets used to harvest the food.

Since the invention of basketry, it would be difficult to separate the history of baskets from food and beverage. Like the question of which came first, the chicken or the egg, you could almost ask the same question about baskets and food. It is unknown how Stone Age man carried seeds to the fields for planting, if he carried them at all. But by the time seeds are actually known to have been planted to raise food for the family, it is believed there were baskets. Not only were the baskets used in planting early on, they were also used in the harvest for hundreds of years.

There was a time when baskets served the same purpose as the large bags from the supermarket. The difference is the baskets were saved and used over and over for years, whereas we usually throw away the bags after the groceries are put away. In those days, there were no supermarkets, only the general store at the crossroads or in the nearby village. Farmers raised most of their foods and bought only staples at the store, so their shopping was not a big chore.

In fact, little of their income went for food bought at the store. Nearly thirty years ago an elderly lady was telling about her life as a girl on a farm. She said her family had a charge account at the nearby country store and paid the bill only once a year—in the fall when crops were gathered and sold. Their annual bill, which included some lengths of fabric, maybe a little ribbon for the girls' hair, and other necessities, was never over one hundred dollars. Usually it was around fifty dollars unless they bought more than they needed, she said.

In the cities it was different. Residents might have a small garden or some fruit trees, but they bought the bulk of their food from the various markets. Few general stores, but many specialized markets like the meat market, the poultry market, the fruit market, and the vegetable market, existed. There was also no refrigeration in those days, which meant that in summer the housewife would take her shopping basket and visit at least some of the markets early every day.

The sellers of the produce also used baskets to display their fruits and vegetables. The housewife selected the things she wanted from their baskets and put them in her basket to take home.

Basketry was also closely associated with beverages, but not totally as with food. Baskets were used early to gather apples to make cider; a universal drink for the first settlers who had been advised not to drink the water. They didn't stop with apple cider; they made perry from pears, peachy from peaches, and wines of all types along with some of the hard stuff—homemade whiskeys from corn.

In the 1890s turnip sellers working on the streets of New York used willow baskets for display.

Around the turn of the century the housewife always took her shopping basket when she went to market.

No doubt about it, some of our ancestors were hearty drinkers, and they cared little whether it was a strong alcoholic beverage or a light one. Shipping beverages from one place to another posed a problem. The glass bottles and jugs were apt to break while being transported by the only means available at that time, a horse- or mule-drawn wagon. There was some river shipping, but it was as hazardous as the wagons. So they devised the basketry-covered bottles and jugs.

This created a new type job, and it must have been more exacting than making a basket. With willow or oak splints, the basketmakers had to cover the bottles and jugs with basketry.

Glass handles were easily broken so they made handles of willow or splints. This handle was easy to use, especially if the owner decided to take it back for a refill.

At that time labor was cheap and covering bottles and jugs with basketry was a smart thing to do. But as labor prices increased and better packaging methods were introduced, it was no longer feasible. However, the fascination about basket-covered bottles and jugs remained, and they continued to be made on a limited scale for years. Basketry-covered bottles of wine from Italy and some South American countries may still be found in stores specializing in imported wines. Wages in those countries have remained miserably low, allowing the wineries to continue using the basket-covered bottles. These jugs and bottles can be found occasionally at flea markets. Apparently, some have been brought home by travelers who were intrigued by the novel bottles.

The basket-covered bottles and jugs were made in this country well into the 1800s, but those early ones are almost impossible to find. The later ones are not as plentiful as you might think, probably because, like the early ones, they were discarded when a better packaging method came along.

The extent of basketry associated with beverages is about covered, with the baskets used to gather the fruits and berries for wines, and the basket-covered bottles and jugs. But bottles of wine were not forgotten. The makers of some picnic baskets remembered to include a round woven holder on the back for the bottles.

The use of the basket in connection with food ran the gamut—from planting to eating. In the early days rural people lived long distances from each other, and had little time for visiting, but most of them went to church regularly. Since they weren't going to work that day, they often took lunch and spent the remainder of the day visiting. This socializing was in addition to the several times a year that dinner-on-the-grounds meetings were held and food was shared with everyone.

The food might be packed in either a covered or an open basket, but it had to be a large one. A large family might take several baskets of food and beverage. Covered baskets were better because they kept out flying insects. Food in the open baskets was simply covered tightly with a snowy white cloth, likely the tablecloth that would be spread over the makeshift tables at lunch. Special baskets were not made for taking food to the churches; they generally filled the ones used for other chores, those that happened to be empty at the time. The low pea baskets were perfect for taking cakes and pies. In fact, some old-timers still call them Sunday cake baskets. Laundry baskets were good for the large containers of food. Later there would be baskets made especially for picnics.

Unlike the baskets used to take food to church, the school lunch basket was made specifically for that purpose and was seldom used for any other. It might be a large, oak, splint basket with a double lid hinged in the center large enough to hold food for all the children in the family, or it might be a small, covered basket, just large enough for one child. Small, open baskets of all types were also used as school lunch baskets. Like those to take food to the church, they were covered with a small, white cloth, usually a napkin.

Remember, there were no movies, no television or radios, not even a quick food place around the turn of the century. About the only place a young man could take his date was on a picnic. Of course, for this he needed a picnic basket, made then in a variety of styles and shapes. Some were empty so the owner could pack whatever he wanted, and others came fitted with essentials such as plates, flatware and maybe glasses.

With the advent of the automobile people began traveling more, perhaps not long distances yet, but more than they had by horseback, stagecoach, or horse and buggy. There were few places to buy a meal so it meant taking food along most of the time. Then there was always the chance the car would have a flat tire, which meant they could be stranded on the road for hours while it was being repaired. Or the car could break down "in the middle of nowhere," as they liked to describe it. Either way it could be hours before they were ready to go again. Perhaps that was one reason some of the cars came equipped with picnic baskets. One shown in the illustrations has the word Renault stamped in the top.

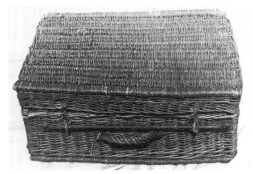

Picnic basket with plain top and rod for fastening.

In recent years, with the trend back to picnics in the park, these old baskets have seen a revival in their uses. Often now, various decorating magazines show how beautiful and useful these old picnic baskets can be, painted white and decorated with bright colors.

Small lunch basket.

Oak splint lunch basket.

New England basket carried food to the church or could be used as a school lunch basket.

Late basketry-covered jug.

Tall basketry-covered bottle.

Picnic basket with design on top and different fasteners.

Inside of basket showing Renault name.

Picnic basket with attached holders for bottles of wine.

Fitted picnic basket.

12

Variations
in Basketry

An old basket may be just another basket to the average person, but to the dedicated collector it is a work of art, nostalgia, a bridge to the past. These collectors can visualize one of the pioneers, perhaps an ancestor, sitting in the shade of a tree in summer, or around the fire on a long winter's night, weaving or coiling a basket. And they are probably right, because the majority of our ancestors, at one time or another, made baskets of some kind. Chances of our getting a basket one of our relatives made is remote. We would probably never know the origin unless the basket was passed down through the family, but it is nice to dream.

Basketry was something anybody and everybody could do, and practically all of them did. Sometimes their baskets were sold to supplement their meager incomes. Or they might make them to replace some that had worn out.

The early settlers as well as many of the later arrivals used their baskets regularly, probably daily. The egg basket is an example. Hardly a housewife alive at that time didn't gather eggs every day—using her egg basket. Other baskets weren't exposed to daily use, but were saved for harder work. They were taken to the fields for both planting and harvesting. After the seeds were planted, the baskets were usually left at the end of the rows where it was easy for the mule, plow, or man to run over them. During the harvest they carried heavy loads.

This wear and tear took its toll on the baskets, as did carrying the heavy loads. Bottoms would rot out of baskets left accidentally in damp places. Any number of reasons caused the baskets to be replaced periodically. Seldom were they used strictly for display or simply for holding a bouquet of flowers as they are today.

The makers regularly made new baskets. If they didn't need them, they could always be sold or given away. Or perhaps their creative juices were flowing, and they just wanted to make something with their hands. What could be easier or less expensive than a basket?

Most baskets, especially those made regionally, are similar. The children were taught by their parents down through the years, so the methods remained basically the same. Regardless of who taught them, the creative ones tried new ideas. This is where some of the differences evolved. Even the older basketmakers varied their work from time to time. It might have been to make a special basket for a gift, or they may have felt they were in a rut and wanted to make their work more interesting or challenging.

Whatever the reason, hundreds of slight variations in baskets have been made in the same style. The biggest difference is probably the way the top was finished and the handle applied. Some used wooden pegs on the handles, others wrapped them with splints, and a few nailed on the handles. In the wrapping lie some of the most interesting differences. Some are wrapped securely. Others have no wrapping at all. The method of wrapping will vary from basket to basket. This is more noticeable in the splint baskets than in the willow or vine, probably because there are so many more examples of splint.

Baskets with different handles.

Some of the differences are so minute it would hardly be noticed by the novice. But as soon as they have collected a dozen or so old baskets with time to study them, even the novice begins to notice small details—the ones that give the baskets so much character and individuality.

Some of the baskets have handles slipped down between two splints and fastened securely. This method was common on utilitarian baskets made to carry heavy loads. For that reason handles were put on firmly so they wouldn't slip out, and hopefully not break. On many of the baskets, handles were made of hickory regardless of the type splints used in the body of the basket. Hickory was tougher and would stand more pressure. It would also bend more readily to ease attachment of the handle. Some of the handles, probably those for heavier things, had handles notched to fit around the splint on top. Handles on the majority of the larger baskets surrounded the basket.

Just as has been done throughout the ages, each craftsman had his own style and methods, but tried to make a serviceable basket according to what he thought was best. As it has been said so many times, our ancestors were opinionated people. If one type handle broke or pulled out while carrying seed to the fields, not only was that a considerable loss, but also they probably refused to make or use another basket with that type handle. Their theory was that if it broke once, it would break again.

So, the next baskets they would make or buy would have a different type handle, probably one that fastened on the basket differently. Basketmakers who made extra income by selling their baskets, were conscious of the likes and dislikes of the buying public. It was ever thus. The maker tries to please his customers. He must, if he plans to continue selling them. Baskets were so generally used that income from them could be rather large in those days, considering the economy. The makers who kept up with changing trends were those who sold the most baskets.

The woven handle is another variation. Baskets with this type handle are not plentiful today, but they are sought-after. Some of the old baskets with plain handles could have had woven handles originally. With excessive use or wear and tear on the handles, the woven part would go first. Then as now, nobody was going to discard a basket just because the woven part of the handle looked ragged. Instead, the worn section was simply cut off, to leave a plain handle.

The difference in handles can be minor. For instance, some baskets might have the center of the handle wider or thicker than on the sides. In other locales there might have been other reasons for this. But one old mountaineer said it was done where he lived so two people could carry the basket at the same time. Apparently this basket carried heavy loads, requiring two women or girls. The wide or thick center section allowed them to grasp either side and easily walk along with the basket.

Other noticeable differences in baskets, usually in the gizzard-shaped or buttocks baskets, are the designs around the top, through the center, and in the bottom. Some might have a double, sometimes a triple, row of wide splints around the top, or the weaving might be a bit fancier around the top. Double splints were also used down the sides and through the bottom, with a fancier weaving design around them. Still another type might have dyed splints mixed with the natural ones to

Crudely made basket with wide and narrow splint design.

Basket with pegged handle.

Similar basket with pegged handle.

Handle fastened in side of basket rather than at top.

Basket with notched handle.

make an elaborate, for a basket, design in the bottom. It might be just brown, walnut-dyed splints mixed with the light, natural-colored ones, or several colors might be used for a particularly beautiful design. Interestingly, as the baskets aged through the years, the colors have also aged so they are not as bright as they were originally. But enough of the colors have remained so the design is still attractive, and the baskets desirable.

In any type of handiwork it is virtually impossible for the worker to make two identical items, human frailties being what they are. They may look the same, but closer examination will reveal small differences the craftsman probably noticed while working on the item. In baskets it might be a wider splint around the top, a wider or taller handle, or it could be the width of the splints used in the basket. It is impossible to cut all the splints exactly the same size without machines, which then removes them from handwork. Actually there were no such machines when the old baskets were being made, hence, the variations.

In coiled baskets the difference could be the size of the coils, or the way they were put together. Those variations are always there, although there are times when they are extremely difficult to find.

Sturdy handle on serviceable basket.

Large basket required only a decorative cross.

Handle secured without the use of excess ties.

Handle left plain.

A simple cross of splints was sufficient for this handle.

Handle goes through the basket.

Well secured handle.

Vine basket with splint tied handle.

Design through center.

Covered handle on basket.

Different design in center.

Three wide strips around top.

Top finished differently.

Plain bottom.

Newly made, oak splint basket.

Bottom most often found.

Old oak splint basket similar to the new one.

Fancy designed bottom.

13

A Basket Is
Merely a Basket

Baskets have always been ignored as an art form. In fact they haven't even been mentioned in connection with art. This would appear somewhat strange considering the possibilities offered by basketry to develop beautiful designs. But somehow the lowly basket has never been closely associated with discussions of designing—or art. The craftsmen simply made the design they thought most fitting, somewhat like the weavers who wove the beautiful designs in the coverlets and in fabric.

"A basket is merely a basket," someone wrote around the turn of the century, "but paint the same design on a piece of vellum, and it acquires instant importance as a work of 'creative imagination.'"

That's true. Few people can describe in detail the design on a basket, but will remember every painting that includes a basket, along with the names of the artists.

It is by no means our intention to suggest that all baskets are great works of art. Quite the contrary, as there are some crude examples, not to mention some that are downright disgraces to the name basket. Most baskets were made with only one thought in the maker's mind—make something useful and durable. There are many beautiful baskets scattered around the country, baskets worthy of admiration, and some that could be classified as artistic. These include the gorgeous Indian-made baskets, especially those of the Western Indians; the plain, but sturdy, Shaker baskets; the Nantucket lightship baskets, and the best of those made by the early settlers, in particular the mountaineers who were skilled basketmakers.

Most early baskets were merely objects to be used, but with a qualifying factor— almost all the makers strived for quality, good workmanship, and design. Some were not as skilled as others. They were unable to make outstanding examples, yet each in his own way made the best he could make, according to his or her ability.

Baskets are still being made today all over the world. Actually basketmaking has never ceased since the first one was made. It may have slowed down at times, but it has never stopped completely. People have always made baskets, and chances are they always will.

Some of the new baskets, especially those of pine-needles, are better quality than those made years ago. Perhaps this is because of greater knowledge, newer methods, and more dedication. Years ago pine-needle basketry was near the bottom of the list of popular basket materials, but recently it has come into its own. It is so popular now that pine-needle basketry is being taught in various craft classes and in junior colleges around the South. It is taught right along with the ever-popular splint basketry. Since prepared materials are now being used in some of the splint baskets, the pine-needle baskets are being made truer to the old methods.

Many of the old basketmakers, with the patience to work with splints cut as fine as thread, are retiring or dying. Those who continue to work have limited the number of baskets they make to a few each year instead of the hundreds they made in past years.

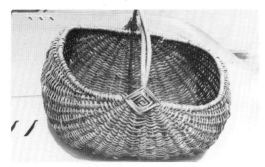

Jamaican-made baskets don't last long because insects destroy them.

Another Jamaican-made basket.

Quality made vine basket.

Indian basketry is also on the wane. One Cherokee basketmaker who feels her people have built a reputation as masters of basketry that should, to quote her, "be carried on as long as the world stands," publicly admits many of the young people in her area won't even try to learn the craft. Other Indian tribes are suffering the same fate.

But there really isn't much cause for alarm. Multitudes of old baskets are still available along with fine quality new ones that are being made everyday. Scarcity has caused prices on old baskets to soar, which in turn has caused many new collectors to accept the fine quality newer baskets.

Some young couples unable to afford the more expensive old baskets have devised some of the most attractive ways to use the newer, fine quality baskets in their homes. For instance, baskets are popular now as plant holders. A person who wouldn't hesitate to use a new fifteen to twenty dollar handmade basket as a plant holder wouldn't consider using a one hundred dollar old one. In the first place, the cost is too high, and secondly, they don't want to risk ruining an old basket in case the liner springs a leak, and the basket is damaged by dampness.

Just as it has always been, there is a collector and a place for all types of baskets and basketry.

Small utility splint basket.

Two sizes of gizzard-shaped or buttocks baskets.

Small basket with old Easter egg for size comparison.

Miniature splint basket.

Larger basket with squared handle.

Small gizzard or buttocks basket made with finer splints.

Medium-sized basket with low handle.

Melon-shaped splint basket.

Two miniatures of different styles.

Honeysuckle vine and splint basket.

Old willow basket.

Vine basket with handles on either side.

Bottom of rye basket.

New England type splint basket.

Serviceable splint basket.

Hickory splint basket.

Serviceable splint basket with low handle.

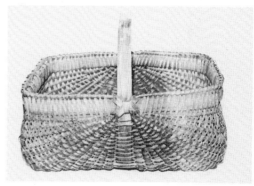

Oak splint basket.

Old splint with tall handle.

95

About the
Author

It would have been impossible for the author to have grown up without a knowledge of and a love for handmade baskets. She had two sets of grandparents who firmly believed "There was a basket for every chore and a chore for every basket." You didn't collect baskets for decorating, you used them. One grandmother even had a beautiful basket she used for storing "plunder," things that didn't fit any place else. As a child she watched the basketmakers make everything from tiny egg baskets to large cotton baskets. Later she taught others to make simple baskets of rattan, but her most interesting basket experience was watching the Cherokee Indians and the older people in the mountains dye the splints and cane with dyes made from natural materials, then weave them into masterpieces.